More Than Enough

More Than Enough

Living Abundantly in a Culture of Excess

LEE HULL MOSES

WESTMINSTER
JOHN KNOX PRESS
LOUISVILLE · KENTUCKY

© 2016 Lee Hull Moses

First edition
Published by Westminster John Knox Press
Louisville, Kentucky

16 17 18 19 20 21 22 23 24 25—10 9 8 7 6 5 4 3 2 1

Book design by Drew Stevens
Cover design by Allison Taylor
Cover illustration: Allison Taylor

Library of Congress Cataloging-in-Publication Data
Names: Moses, Lee Hull, author.
Title: More than enough : living abundantly in a culture of excess / Lee Hull Moses.
Description: First edition. I Louisville, KY : Westminster John Knox Press, [2016] I Description based on print version record and CIP data provided by publisher; resource not viewed.
Identifiers: LCCN 2016020340 (print) I LCCN 2016013582 (ebook) I ISBN 9781611647648 (ebk.) I ISBN 9780664261283 (pbk. : alk. paper)
Subjects: LCSH: Wealth--Religious aspects--Christianity. I Christianity--United States.
Classification: LCC BR115.W4 (print) I LCC BR115.W4 M67 2016 (ebook) I DDC 241/.68--dc23
LC record available at https://lccn.loc.gov/2016020340

Most Westminster John Knox Press books are available at special quantity discounts when purchased in bulk by corporations, organizations, and special-interest groups. For more information, please e-mail SpecialSales@wjkbooks.com.

For Rob

He has brought down the powerful from their thrones,
  and lifted up the lowly;
he has filled the hungry with good things,
  and sent the rich away empty.

—Luke 1:52–53

Again I tell you, it is easier for a camel to go through the eye of a needle than for someone who is rich to enter the kingdom of God.

—Matthew 19:24

I came that they may have life, and have it abundantly.

—John 10:10

CONTENTS

ACKNOWLEDGMENTS

———— ⬭⬭ ————

Many of these words were fueled by the good coffee and amazing pumpkin chocolate chip muffins at Spring Garden Bakery. If you find yourself in Greensboro, North Carolina, you should stop in.

The Louisville Institute provided funding for me to step away from church life for a while and work on this project. That is a gift I do not take for granted.

The folks at St. Francis Springs Prayer Center offered me gracious hospitality and enabled me to get a lot of writing done by not providing Internet access to guests.

I am grateful for old friends who live too far away but are still easy to laugh with, whose lives and work inspire me, and whose insights found their way into these pages in a number of ways. Thanks, Julie Phillips, Becca Evans, and Brenda O'Connell.

Laura Jean Torgerson and Tim Donaghy were friends and conversation partners long before they opened their Nicaraguan home to me. I am grateful for their friendship and their hospitality.

Bromleigh McCleneghan and Katherine Willis Pershey are friends and writing partners who helped me figure out how to turn a question into a book. Many other people helped this book come to life by sharing conversations, reading drafts, and offering encouragement: Diane Faires, David Fraccaro, Alisa Roadcup, Amy Gopp, Sandhya Jha, Rebecca Todd Peters, Ramsey and Kevin McIntire, Nathan Dungan, Taylor McCleneghan, Melissa Guthrie, Heidi Haverkamp, Jenn Moland-Kovash, Erica Schemper, Ginny Inman, Marti Hazelrigg, Jo Owens, Sarah Carver, and members of First Congregational Church in Norwood, Massachusetts.

Jessica Miller Kelley offered support and encouragement (and kept me from including too many parenthetical asides) throughout the writing process.

Beth Gaede lent her editorial wisdom at a number of stages during the writing of this book, reminding me to always make my antecedents clear.

Lindsey Altvater Clifton wrestled messy chapter drafts into a well-formatted manuscript.

My parents, Rick and Linda Hull, and my sister, Lynn Hull, read drafts, babysat while I wrote, talked through ideas, and let me tell their stories.

The good, faithful people of First Christian Church (Disciples of Christ) in Greensboro gave me time and space for writing and took good care of my family. They inspire me, challenge me, and give me hope. It is a joy to be their pastor.

Jonathan and Harper want me to read books with them, which is way better than ever writing my own. Rob makes my ministry and writing possible in myriad ways, not the least of which is the way he smiles at me when I come in the door.

I am grateful.

INTRODUCTION

The morning is marked by the sounds of rain on the roof and the tantrums of an overtired little boy who did not sleep well, which means that none of us did. His big sister is a good sport, though, and gets herself ready for school without complaining. She folds up her umbrella neatly when she steps on the bus, like a grown-up kid heading out into the world.

Intermingled with the rain and the tantrum and the getting ready is a radio story about the Rwandan genocide. It was playing in the background as I coaxed Harper out of bed and helped her pick out her school clothes. They were still talking about it when I got the kids settled in the kitchen and came back to get dressed myself. It's at least the third reference to Rwanda I've heard in the last few days, so it must be that this is an anniversary—the twentieth, I gather (when did I get old enough to remember things that happened twenty years ago?)—but I keep missing the beginning of the story and the context.

I remember Rwanda. I was in college when I heard an interview on National Public Radio with Philip Gourevitch, the author of *We Wish to Inform You That Tomorrow We Will Be Killed with Our Families,* a book that had brought the atrocities of genocide to the public's attention. I had just started listening to NPR; I'd always thought of it as something boring my dad listened to in the car and had just recently discovered that it might be relevant to me. The title of the book alone made me order it, but I read only part of it, enough to get a sense of the story and how terrible it was. Enough to know that I couldn't bear to read any more.

As the kids eat breakfast on this rainy morning, I wonder, and not for the first time: How is it that these things exist in the same world? The horrors of genocide, children murdered and worse as their families watch, while my family's greatest problem this morning is that nobody brought up the laundry from the basement, so we can't find any clean socks. How can it be that my kitchen is full of good and healthy food—so much of it that our quandary about what to have for dinner tonight will be one of too many choices, not too few—while some 25 percent of children in my state alone don't know where their next meal will come from? How can there be so much delight and beauty and so much pain and brokenness?

How can these two realities exist in the same God-created world?

And how—given that they do—are we supposed to live?

That is, how do we live, my family and I—and maybe yours—in a way that honors God and shows gratitude for the good life we are living, in the midst of a world where genocide happens, where there are hungry people in our own communities while food rots in grocery store trash cans, where workers can't make enough to take care of their families, where people work long hours in unsafe working conditions to build the very computer I am typing on?

How do we live?

Now, if you picked up this book in the first place—and presumably no one is forcing you to read it—then you probably have some inkling about what I'm talking about. You probably know that the gap between rich and poor is getting bigger all the time and that people in the United States make up a small percentage of the world's population but use a hugely disproportionate amount of the world's resources. By almost any measure, the United States is the richest country in the world.

When it comes to individual people, though, there's no good definition of "rich." We could use the government's definition of poverty, but of course, that doesn't mean much, because a lot of families who make more than that still struggle to get by.

So, I can't really tell you if you're rich or not. I can't tell you if you ought to be reading this book or not. I'm not going to try to convince you that you're better off than you think you are. Because I know: you've got student loans and car payments, and child care costs as much as college tuition, and you're underwater on your mortgage, and your spouse didn't get that raise you were expecting, and the only thing that shows up in your mailbox anymore is bills. It doesn't feel like you're rich. I know.

But consider this: If you could afford to buy this book and have time to read it . . . if you own more than one technological device that requires a charger . . . if you've got a safe place to sleep tonight . . . if you know what you're having for dinner or at least you know you can afford dinner . . . if you've got even a little savings to fall back on, if you're starting to think about how you'll put your kids through college, if you've eaten in a restaurant this week or swung through a drive-through . . . then I'm going to go out on a limb and say that you've got more than most people in the world.

Me, too.

We're doing OK, my family and me. We've got two full-time jobs that pay us reasonably and provide our health insurance. We've been lucky in some ways. Frugal and strategic in others. My parents made some investments when I was little that paid off well. My parents were lucky, frugal, and strategic, too—and thanks to scholarships along the way, I didn't have to use all of it for school. Our kids are generally healthy, we've been able to find work we're qualified for and enjoy, and we've thus far avoided any natural or human-made disasters. Some might use the word "blessed" here, but I hesitate to do so—not because I don't feel blessed; I do, absolutely. But things get a little squishy when I start to talk about the good things in my life as *blessings*. Because what about people who don't have as much as I do? Or who've been hit by those disasters, big and small, that we've managed to miss? Have they not been blessed? Does God not care about them?

See? It gets complicated quick.

Here, of course, is where we have to talk about privilege, and I'll be up front that I've got a lot of it: I'm white, so there's that. I had access to a good education. I'm straight—my relationship with my partner has never been up for public debate. Rob and I married while I was still in graduate school, early in our careers, which means we get the tax breaks, and we've always had two people paying the rent or the mortgage. I'm Christian, which, despite the rapid decline in church attendance, is still the country's dominant religion.

About the only nonprivileged category I can claim is that I'm a woman, and I have to tell you—and I know this isn't true for everybody—in my family, in my church, that hasn't been much of a problem.

Even the writing of this book is a privilege; I have a job that offers me a paid sabbatical from work—paid time off to read and write and think. This is a rare and treasured gift.

So now, I'm guessing, you would sort of like to put the book down, because I sound kind of obnoxious and braggy about all my privilege and everything I've got and how easy my life is . . .

And you'd be right, I guess—though I don't mean to be obnoxious and braggy about it. I have a lot, and my life thus far has been pretty easy. If it would help, I could tell you some not-so-wonderful things about my life, like how we sometimes have mice in our silverware drawer. I could tell you about the time I accidentally put diesel fuel into my gas tank and had to spend a fair chunk of change to drain it out. I could tell you how we screwed up our taxes a while back and ended up owing *a lot*. I could tell you that I unreasonably can't let it go how Rob never shuts the closet door or how sometimes we snap at each other for no reason except that we're tired.

You'd also be right to call me a hypocrite, because hypocrisy is inevitable in a conversation like this. I'm writing about making responsible choices with our money, living faithfully with what we have, being mindful of where our stuff comes from and what kind of impact we have on the world around us . . . and in a minute I'm going to get up, throw away my disposable coffee cup, check the messages on my iPhone, and then drive my car a reasonably walkable distance to my house.

I'm not perfect. It's not easy. There are no simple answers here.

But I'm hoping you'll stick with me, because nobody's life is perfect or simple or easy.

Here are some things I know to be true:

I know that the gospel of Jesus Christ offers good news for the poor and oppressed. That's the Bible story, over and over again: God lifts up the downtrodden, gives new life, renews the covenant, keeps the promise. That's the hope our faith offers us: a vision of a restored, redeemed, transformed world. I know that.

I know that this is a really, really broken world. There is far too much injustice and far too much need.

I know that my life — my home, my family, my work — is good and sweet and (dare I say?) holy.

I know that I can't ignore the broken world just because my life is good, and also—though this has taken a longer time coming—I know that just because the world is broken doesn't mean I can't enjoy my good, sweet, holy life.

I know that sometimes I'm part of the problem.

I know that something has to change.

For those of us who want to do something, the response to the problem of how we live faithfully with abundance falls onto a sort of spectrum. We could decide not to respond at all. We could just go about our lives without worrying about it, not feeling guilty, not making any changes. That's a tempting choice, because the needs of the world are awfully overwhelming, and most of the time it doesn't feel like we have much power to do anything about it.

But if that's not sufficient for you, one response is to completely disengage from the system entirely. We could recognize that our buying habits, our consumption, all our choices are hurting the earth and our neighbors, so we could opt out. We could move to a farm, raise our own food, sew our own clothes, and generally go off the grid, thereby limiting our carbon footprint and impacting our neighbors only by sharing the occasional basket of just-laid chicken eggs. Maybe that sounds good to you, and maybe you have the resources and know-how to do it.

Here's why it doesn't work for me: I don't know how to make my own clothes, and I don't have much of a green thumb, and I'm much better at working with people and words than I am with plants and animals. Plus, there's this: As followers of Jesus, we are called to live *in* the world and engage it, not withdraw from it completely. Escaping is not the answer.

A second response is to be moved to compassion by the suffering in the world. We see a need, we know that we have a lot, and we give away some of what we have.

We send our money to causes we believe in, we buy extra food at the grocery store and drop it off at the food pantry, we donate our old clothes to Goodwill. That's all good. It is a good and generous thing to donate food and money and clothes. But it doesn't go quite far enough, because if we donate food for hungry people in our community, we must also ask why there are so many hungry people in our community in the first place. And if we give away our old clothes and then go out and buy new clothes, shouldn't we pay attention to where those clothes are made and find out what kind of working conditions they were made in?

Don't get me wrong: I hope that we'll live generously and give away a lot—and not just the stuff we don't need (is it really generosity or sacrifice to give away a pair of jeans that doesn't fit you anymore?), not just from the pennies left over at the end of the month, but the firstfruits at the beginning.

The reality, though, is that most of us are not going to figure out how to live completely self-sustainably. Nor are we going to give away everything we own. Most of us still need to buy groceries and shoes for our kids and clothes for ourselves. Most of us will need a car, and most families need two. We'll need to buy dish soap and laundry baskets, and sometimes we'll go out to eat. We're going to think about saving some money for our kids' education or for our retirement, and if we're fortunate to have a little extra, maybe we'll want to do something fun, like take a vacation or remodel our bathroom.

That's a lot of decisions, and they all matter. These are big, complicated questions about justice and economics and generosity and advocacy and globalization. So how do we make faithful choices in all those everyday tasks of living in the world? I'm not going to tell you what choices to make or how to live. I'll tell you what I've learned and what my family has tried—and sometimes what we've been meaning to try but haven't. I'll point us toward some resources and practices from the Christian tradition that will prove helpful, and we'll look to the Scriptures, because those ancient words just may be the best hope we've got.

I promise not to scold too much (or, if I do, I'll be on the receiving end of the scolding right there with you). I promise not to drown you in statistics. I promise not to offer all the answers. At the end of this book, I'm afraid we'll still have more stuff than we need and the world will still be broken. But I do think there are some things we can do. I think there must be a faithful way to live. There is good news for all of us.

∞◯∞

A word about how this book is set up: For the most part, the odd-numbered chapters are a little more practical. That is, they examine hands-on topics like money, possessions, community service, and advocacy work. The even-numbered chapters are more theoretical; they explore ideas and practices that Christians have used for centuries to make sense of their lives and their relationship with God. All the chapters ultimately ask the question: *How should we live?*

You'll find Scripture woven throughout these pages, along with conversations I've had with friends, colleagues, and other smart people I know only through reading their books. My family shows up here from time to time as well, so allow me to introduce them:

My daughter, Harper, is in elementary school. She loves science experiments and Junie B. Jones books (despite my repeated encouragement to try Harry Potter) and board games of just about any kind. She's got enough attitude to make me a wee bit nervous about her teenage years, but she's also clever and brave and kind and funny.

Jonathan—my preschooler—is, in a term I kind of hated until I had one of my own, *all boy.* He smashes into things—walls, chairs, his sister—for no apparent reason and likes to shout at the top of his lungs, after which he usually grins at me and says calmly, "I'm yelling!" He is slightly obsessed with the moon.

Rob, my husband and partner for more than a decade now, is an IT guy. He's good at what he does because he's good with people; he can explain what's wrong with your computer without using too much technospeak, and then— !!—he can fix it. He and I recently passed the point at which we've been part of each other's lives longer than we weren't. He's nicer to me than I deserve, but I'm learning that that's what marriage—and grace—seem to be about.

I'm really grateful for my life. I bet you are grateful for yours. There is a way to live that honors that gratitude and moves us to a deeper engagement with the world around us. Let's see if we can find it.

CHAPTER 1

--- ⌒⌒ ---

LIVE IT WELL

Building Houses and Hanging Hammocks

A piece of advice: if you are lucky enough to have a friend with a hammock in a tropical part of the world, and said friend invites you to visit her and ponder the great questions of life while swinging in the hammock, you should take her up on it.

My trip to Nicaragua starts the day after Ash Wednesday, just as the season of Lent begins. At church the night before I leave, with our foreheads smeared with ashes, a friend tells me he's always loved Ash Wednesday, but he can't quite articulate why. There's something "darkly beautiful," he says. I agree: to acknowledge the complete inevitability of death is reassuring. We need not try so hard to avoid it.

I'm keenly aware of my own mortality as I say good-bye to my children and leave the country for the first time since they were born. I won't be gone that long, less than a week, and Nicaragua is an easy flight from Miami, but it feels very far away. I leave midmorning; the kids are at school and Rob's at work, so I write them each notes to leave on their pillows.

I get to the airport early and stop at the bookstore before getting in line for security. I have absolutely no need for another book — I have at least three with me — but last night I told Rob what I planned to bring to read and he said, "Those all sound boring; you should take something fun." He is probably right. There isn't a novel in the collection. I look for a while at the airport bookstore, but I can't find anything that meets my primary criteria; that is, a book that costs less than ten dollars and that I'm sure I will like. I contemplate a magazine, but the easy-to-read stuff will just make me feel bad about the state of my social life/body/hair/house/parenting skills, and the *New Yorker* just offers more of the heady stuff I already have in my carry-on. As it turns out, it doesn't matter; I sleep most of the way to Miami and then to Managua.

My friend Laura Jean and her family — her husband, Tim, and their daughters, Quinn and Maya — have lived in Nicaragua for the past several years. She's a minister, and they've been serving as missionaries with Global Ministries, the joint mission effort of the Christian Church (Disciples of Christ) and the United Church of Christ. They're partnered with a Nicaraguan denomination called La Misión Cristiana. Laura Jean has been teaching theology at the local seminary and started a program for rural church members who want to become pastors but don't have access to education. Tim is a scientist, a physicist. He's also been teaching classes in environmental studies at the university.

Plus — I think this is amazing and I keep making him explain it to me — Tim has spent a whole lot of time working with volunteers from the local church to build biodigesters for churches in rural areas. If you think a biodigester is something out of a science fiction story, you're not far off.

It's a contraption that turns cow manure into methane gas, in a way that cuts down on odor and pollution and makes the gas safe for indoor cooking. In parts of the country that have a lot of cows and not many trees—thanks to decades of deforestation—a biodigester makes fuel from a widely available resource that otherwise would be a disposal problem. It is a lot safer and more energy efficient than a wood-burning stove. (When I tell this story to someone back at home, she misunderstands me and thinks that Tim is helping people cook with cow manure. Like, in the pan with their rice and beans. Um, no.)

Tim and Laura Jean are awesome. I've come to visit not just because they're doing such good work here but also because they're good friends. Laura Jean and I were pregnant together with our firstborns; we happened to live in the same place then, so we compared notes on swollen ankles, went to prenatal yoga together, and took long walks with our newborns in their strollers. Those are the kinds of friendships that stick, even when one of you moves to a place you need a passport to get to.

Laura Jean's hammock is on the front porch of their house, and she's right: it's a good place for pondering life's great questions. It's also a good place to take a nap, or to read a book to one of the girls, or to listen to the neighbors laughing. Quinn and I spend quite a bit of time in the hammock together; she has a notebook and pencil and she's writing a story about the richest family in the world, with fourteen daughters who all live in a palace.

One night, we're invited to dinner at the home of some friends of Laura Jean and Tim's. They are expats as well, having come to Nicaragua to work for a faith-based social service agency a decade ago. Somewhere along the way, they decided to make their lives here; they have two children and a house up in the hills above Managua.

When we arrive, Paul is hanging up socks on an elaborate clothesline suspended from the ceiling of the porch. His wife, Becca, tells us that the water had just been delivered; their house is built at the end of a long, winding road, and there's no infrastructure here. They have the water carted up by oxen two or three times a week.

Paul and Becca built this house themselves. It's a straw-bale house, which is exactly what it sounds like: the walls are built out of straw bales covered with plaster. The straw bales make for excellent insulation and are more sustainable than other construction materials. (I manage to bite my tongue long enough to avoid making the obvious "three little pigs" joke.) I know people in the States who have built their own houses, and I am always amazed. That one could know enough to actually construct a dwelling place for one's family astounds me. I'm not even any good at building a fort out of couch cushions in the living room.

I'm feeling very much like a tourist as I marvel at all the eccentricities of their house, which is beautiful and well built. It's not big, but it has everything a house needs, and the big porch and hillside give the sense that the home doesn't end at the straw-filled walls. Their doors and windows don't lock, and they hire a neighbor to stay nearby as security all the time. In their upstairs loft bedroom, a door-sized window opens out to a second-story deck that overlooks the cascading hillside below. Conspicuously, there is no railing.

"We had one, but it broke, and we just never replaced it," Becca tells me as I take a step back, away from the edge, my acrophobia kicking me in the stomach. "It's nicer for doing yoga up here, without the railing in the way of the view, and the kids just know to be careful."

I try not to be too obnoxiously interested in every little detail of their lives, but I'm intrigued by this family that looks just like mine but lives so differently. We take a walk to the orchard, and Becca picks a fruit I've never heard of. Back at the house, she squeezes it into a pitcher with water and a little sugar. We drink it at room temperature, but it's still a relief from the afternoon heat.

The girls are excited about the prospect of a dip in the hot tub after dinner. When Laura Jean mentioned the hot tub before we arrived, I had a moment of self-righteous gloating. *They have a hot tub? How sustainable can that be?* I thought, imagining the electricity needed to heat the huge tarp-covered tubs in suburban American backyards. It turns out, however, that this hot tub is a six-foot half circle of cement, the size of a large bathtub, built by Paul when he was building the walls of the house. It's heated by a fire he stokes every once in a while as we are chatting on the patio. It may be a luxury, this handmade hot tub, but it is no energy-guzzling plastic monstrosity.

During dinner, we get to talking about children. Watching the girls makes me miss my own kids, and I wonder what they are doing at home right now. Paul and Becca moved to this house shortly before their older daughter was born, so it is the only home their girls have ever known. They are Nicaraguans. Talk turns to the details of child rearing, and some things don't vary by culture: Maya isn't quite ready to be potty trained, but Laura Jean is thinking about it. Becca tells us that the nice thing about this house is the cement floors; it makes for easy cleanup when one of her girls doesn't make it to the bathroom in time.

I mention that we tried potty training with Jonathan a while back, but he wasn't really into it, so we'll try again in few months. I tell them that I've been waiting to replace our living room rug; it's been peed on so many times that it really just needs to be burned. I say this as a way to connect to the conversation—*Yes! Potty training is messy! The floor is a disaster!*—but as soon as it's out of my mouth, I realize how American this makes me sound: even our home furnishings are disposable. I'm visiting a family who recycles their washing-machine water, and I'm talking nonchalantly about throwing away my rug.

They aren't showing off, and they aren't judging me; this is just the way they live their lives. This is the sort of intentional living I long for, I realize with a confused mix of jealousy and relief, but in my mind my life doesn't look at all like this. I don't want to live in the hills of Managua; I don't want my water to have to be brought up the hill by oxen; I don't have the know-how or the desire to build my own house, no matter how sustainable it might be. This is a good and faithful life, I'm sure; it's just not mine.

My life, at least for these years, is in North Carolina, in a house in a leafy neighborhood, on a street that's a little bit too busy for Jonathan to play freely in the front yard. It's an old house and not particularly energy efficient, though we did install better windows, and we try not to overdo it with the heat or air-conditioning. There are things we could and should do better in the choices we make and the impact we have on our poor, neglected earth.

But the reality is that, for better or worse, my life is here in the United States. Becca and Paul have built their lives in Nicaragua, and Tim and Laura Jean have made their home there for a season. To be able to visit them there is a gift, but that's not my life.

The words of Jeremiah 29 keep coming to mind. The prophet is writing to the exiled Israelites who find themselves in Babylon, and they are coming to realize that they're not going to get home to Jerusalem any time soon.

> Build houses and settle down; cultivate gardens and eat what they produce. Get married and have children; then help your sons find wives and your daughters find husbands in order that they too may have children. Increase in number there so that you don't dwindle away. Promote the welfare of the city where I have sent you into exile. Pray to the Lord for it, because your future depends on its welfare.
>
> —Jer. 29:5–7 CEB

"Build houses and settle down," says the Lord, through the voice of the prophet. Grow gardens and have families. This is where your life is now.

It's not exactly the same, I realize. I'm hardly in exile here, in my comfortable house, in a town of my own choosing. But it's where my life is now.

Maybe that's what I've been wrestling with: figuring out where God is calling me to live my life and then figuring out how to live it well. To live in a way that honors my gratitude for the life I have. To celebrate the diversity of life on this globe. To do good where I am, to "promote the welfare of the city" where I've made my life. To pay attention to the choices I make and the impact I have on the earth and the people around me. To delight in the goodness and sweetness of this life.

The way that I do that will be different from the way you do it, which will be different from Becca and Paul, and Laura Jean and Tim. There are lots of ways: Some folks have decided to give away everything they have and live in intentional poverty so that they can better stand in solidarity with the poor. Some are philanthropists who manage their wealth in such a way that they can support important work in their community. Some are imagining new family structures and creating communal living arrangements in which they share what they have.

There are a lot of faithful ways to live this life, to live responsibly and gratefully with the abundance of gifts we've been given. But there are also some not-so-faithful ways to live. There are, even, some sinful ways to live. To live without gratitude. To live selfishly. To live as if we are entitled to what we have or as if we've earned it all ourselves. To live without any sort of regard for the people with whom we share this earth.

I don't want to live like that. I want to live the most faithful, most grace-filled, most life-giving life I can.

On my first full day in Nicaragua, we stop at a market, and I buy small souvenirs for the kids. I don't usually do that when I travel—they have no need for more stuff— but an out-of-the-country trip feels like it calls for different rules. I get a small ball for Jonathan and maracas for

Harper. I also, with an impulsiveness I don't usually have, buy a hammock. It's red and white, the loose rope kind with two big rings but no bar at each end, so it'll fit into my suitcase going home. We have two trees in our backyard that I've always thought would be the perfect distance apart for a hammock.

When I get home, we rig it up with clips and ropes, and as the winter finally wanes, it hangs as a reminder of the hot Managua breeze. Life moves on, much as before, but every once in a while, I glance out the back window while I'm washing the dishes and the hammock catches my eye. I think of Paul and Becca's hand-built straw-bale house, and our beloved, drafty home. I think of the water that comes straight from the faucet in my kitchen sink, and the water they so carefully ration. I think of all the ways we make the best lives we can, right where we are. Spring finds us in the backyard more and more, and I often catch Harper out there with a book, one leg hanging out of the hammock to keep it swinging.

CHAPTER 2

────── ∽∞∞ ──────

ENOUGH

One Sunday evening back in January, a small parable played itself out, mostly unnoticed, at the downtown ice skating rink. The night we were there was warm; we barely needed jackets, and the ice kept turning to slush, making skating difficult. But for kids in a town that gets only one or two sled-quality snows a year, this artificial rink and the sledding hill nearby were a big hit.

After Harper had connected with some of her friends from school and was getting her balance on actual ice skates, I took Jonathan—still a little too small for the rink—to check out the sleds.

The hill was as popular as the ice rink, even if it wasn't much in the grand scheme of sledding hills. It was more of an icy ramp with a six-foot rise that kids slid down on thick plastic saucers provided by the management. When we got there, there was a long line of kids waiting on the stairs leading to the top, and another group of kids and parents milling around at the bottom of the stairs, trying to figure out the system.

Each of the kids standing on the stairs leading to the top of the hill had a sled, but there didn't seem to be any more available. Where do you get the sleds? we asked each other and looked around, confused. A few people walked to the far end of the hill where the slope ended and lay in wait for exiting sledders. Others hung around the bottom of the stairs until someone showed up with a sled. There were more than a few almost-harsh words: "That's mine!" "I was waiting!" I could feel the anxiety level of the crowd rising, as everyone jostled to get their hands on this suddenly scarce and highly valuable commodity.

Finally, the worker at the top of the stairs hollered down, "Pass up the sleds!" Those of us holding sleds looked around for a few minutes, confused. We'd waited for these sleds! Fought for them! Earned them! And we were supposed to just pass them on, before we got a chance to use them?

But then it finally clicked: there *weren't* enough sleds for everyone standing in line to hold one. But you didn't need a sled if you were just standing in line. You only needed a sled when you got to the top and were ready to go down, and by then, a sled would have been passed up to you from the waiting people below. There were more than enough sleds.

Eventually, it began to work. Kids coming off the hill carried their sleds around to the stairs and passed them off, then joined the end of the line, sledless, until someone else passed a sled up to them. No one ever reached the top without a sled. Everybody got a turn.

When it worked, it worked, but the system ebbed and flowed. Whenever someone new showed up, someone who hadn't yet figured out the process, the anxiety level rose again and the system got all out of whack, with people grabbing for sleds, jostling for slots, fearful that they wouldn't get a turn, and so hanging on for dear life to a sled that wasn't going anywhere.

∽◌∾

After the Hebrew people cross the Red Sea, out of slavery and into the wilderness, they have to figure out how to live as the free people of God. For generations—longer than any of them can remember—they'd not been free; they'd been enslaved in Pharaoh's economy of scarcity. As Old Testament scholar Walter Brueggemann describes it, they'd been cogs in a system that convinced them that the goal was more work, more production, more everything. There was never enough.[1]

Those of us who live in twenty-first-century North America—where we are bombarded with thousands of advertising images a day, all trying to persuade us that we need *something*—know well that scarcity is a hard worldview to leave behind. I'm guessing that when those slaves dreamt about not being slaves anymore, they imagined that freedom meant they would finally get to enjoy all that *more.* But what they discover out in the wilderness—what God needs them to learn before they can grow up and be God's people—is that freedom from slavery doesn't mean access to *more, more, more.* It means they will have enough.

> The whole congregation of the Israelites complained against Moses and Aaron in the wilderness. The Israelites said to them, "If only we had died by the hand of the LORD in the land of Egypt, when we sat by the fleshpots and ate our fill of bread; for you have brought us out into this wilderness to kill this whole assembly with hunger."
>
> Then the LORD said to Moses, "I am going to rain bread from heaven for you, and each day the people shall go out and gather enough for that day."
>
> —Exod. 16:2–4

Enough for that day.

No more, no less; enough. The Israelites aren't any better at gathering *enough* manna than we were at trusting that there were enough sleds for everybody who wanted a turn. To a people who were so recently slaves, who had to grovel and beg for every scrap of food, walking past fresh bread scattered on the ground seems inconceivable (even if the bread came mysteriously from heaven and they can't quite identify it — manna translates nicely as "what is it?"). They gather more than they need, and it rots. There was enough manna. There were enough sleds to go around.

Such a tricky word, *enough.* So hard to define, so hard to put a pin in and hold down.

One friend tells me that he and his wife have talked about what their optimal combined income would be. They both work hard in executive-level, nonprofit careers, though not high-paying ones. There's a line they don't want to go above, he says — partly because they're always aware of the gigantic gap between their own income and that of the people they serve in their work but also because, he said, at some point, that'll be enough.

Enough.

∞∞∞

Centuries after the manna appeared to the whining Israelites, and centuries before the parable of the sledding hill, Jesus gives his disciples a lesson in God's enough. They look at the crowds on the hillside, all those thousands of people who have come to hear Jesus, and they can't imagine how they all will be fed. *There will never be enough.* But, of course, there is.

> Taking the five loaves and the two fish, he looked up to heaven, and blessed and broke the loaves, and gave them to his disciples to set before the people; and he divided the two fish among them all. And all ate and were filled; and

they took up twelve baskets full of broken pieces and of the fish.

—Mark 6:41–43

Freedom of the sort God offers the Israelites on the other side of the Red Sea—the same sort of freedom Jesus offers the crowds on the hillside and you and me, too—that sort of freedom is dependent on the recognition that life with God is not a zero-sum game. More for you does not mean less for me. Five baskets of food fed five thousand people and generated twelve baskets of leftovers. Regular math does not apply here.

It's not a competition.

It's normal, we tell ourselves, to want the best for our children, for our families. For these people we love most in the world, we want nothing but the best. Not mediocre, not just OK. Even if we're able to get past our desire for the material "bests"—OK, so maybe my kid doesn't need the *best* bike on the market—we still want the best schools, the best opportunities, the best *whatever.*

But here's the thing about superlatives such as "best," "most," and all those words that end in "-est." The fastest swimmer, the strongest player, the smartest student in the class . . . We start competing.

Not everybody can be the best. Not everybody can have the most.

But everybody can have enough.

When Jesus passed around those baskets of bread and fish, not everybody got the best cut of fish, the biggest chunk of bread. But based on the amount of leftovers gathered up afterward, apparently everybody had enough.

The best is a limited commodity in an economy of scarcity. Pharaoh demands more production, more bricks, more labor. The disciples say, "There's not enough food." The Israelites gather up more manna than they need and are surprised when it rots.

We fight for a sled when there are plenty to go around.

More asks: What else can I get?
Enough asks: Do I really need more?

I want my kids to have enough. I want my family to have enough. And I want everybody else to have enough, too.

What would my dinner tonight look like if what I wanted was enough? What would my closet look like? My bank account? My car?

What would our schools look like if we wanted enough for our kids? What would our public policies for hunger relief look like if we wanted enough?

God does not want the Israelites to starve. They have not come all this way to simply perish in the wilderness. Jesus does not want the crowds on the hillside to go hungry. God does not call us to lives of want.

God calls us to lives of enough.

Enough is not nothing.

Enough has no winners or losers.

No one goes hungry, and no one gets lost.

Enough, with grace, is abundant life.

CHAPTER 3

———— ∞⚬∞ ————

THE COMPLICATED
LIFE

Simple Living Just Isn't

After I dropped Jonathan off at school this morning, I stopped by the farmers' market. We were out of town last weekend, so I'd missed my usual Saturday morning visit and needed to stock up on some veggies. The Wednesday market isn't as bustling or as full as it is on Saturday, but I found everything I needed, plus some: a big bag of kale (I know, it's so trendy right now: I'm cool like that), some green leaf lettuce, a couple of tomatoes, and the heaven in a bucket known as a gallon of freshly picked strawberries.

North Carolina in the spring is amazing. Actually, I love North Carolina in the summer and fall, too. It's only January that I don't really like; but I'm not sure I'd like January anywhere. Anyway, food grows well here this time of year;

it's lush and green and abundant, and there's really no reason to ever eat produce shipped from someplace else.

Backyard gardens—and front-yard gardens, for that matter—are everywhere, and there's a huge network of community gardens in town. The garden ministry at our church is going strong, now in its sixth season. I've noticed a growing awareness in my community and across the country that our food systems have got to change, and more and more people are eating locally and growing their own food. This is all very good.

Some of us who make our lives in North America are coming to realize that the way we are living just isn't sustainable. We're taxing the world's human and natural resources at a rate that isn't good for us, our neighbors, or the earth. Food and all the related buzzwords—local, organic, natural, whole—are one piece of the puzzle, but there's also all the energy we use to heat and cool our houses, run our cars, and power all our electronic equipment. There's the clothes we wear, where and how they're made, the working conditions of the people who make them, and the sheer volume of clothes in our closets. Or the trash we produce. Turns out that guy from the movie *The Graduate* was right when he promised a young Dustin Hoffman that the future was in plastics. Little did he know that we'd be almost drowning in it. (My sister tells me that her husband occasionally suggests building an addition to their house to store their empty Tupperware.)

The truth is, we aren't treating our earth, our bodies, or our neighbors very well.

☙❧

Several years ago, before we had kids, Rob and I made a visit to my aunt and uncle, who live in a lovely little town on the coast of Maine. It's everything you think of when you hear "lovely little town on the coast of Maine"—it's quaint, and there are boats in the harbor, seafood restaurants galore, and an ice cream parlor. We watched the boats, ate ice cream, and browsed the souvenir shops.

In one sweet little shop, full of T-shirts and postcards and lobster-themed gifts (many of which, in later years, would find their way via my aunt into my children's collections), I found a rack of bumper stickers that read, "Live Simply So That Others Might Simply Live."[1] It wasn't exactly a new concept to me, though I don't think I'd heard that particular phrase before, and it caught my eye and my imagination. I bought it, and not being one to put bumper stickers on my car, I propped it up on a bookshelf in my office when I got home.

That was late summer 2006. Harper was born eleven months later, and I'm pretty sure that nothing has ever been simple since.

∞∞∞

I've developed a certain image in my mind of what a family living the "simple life" looks like. It's one giant, unfair caricature, but here it is:

The family car (and yes, there's only one) is a small, fuel-efficient model, a little beat-up because it's been around for so long. It's old, but it still runs well enough. When it finally dies, they plan to look into a car with an electric motor.

The car doesn't get used that often, though, because of course they ride their bikes or walk most places. The parents work from home, in a studio they converted themselves from the old garage. The kids go to school in the neighborhood. The backyard (which gets just the right mixture of sun and shade) is a full garden, complete with a fruit tree, and the front yard is landscaped in such a way that it requires neither watering nor mowing. There are solar panels on the roof and a rain barrel at the corner of the house. They raise chickens and eat fresh eggs every morning. The kids play outside all day, forgoing toxin-laden sunscreen yet magically never get sunburned.

No plastic is allowed in their home; food is stored in canning jars, and even the kids drink out of real glass (which of course is never dropped and broken on the original, restored hardwood floor). The pantry is full of canned beans from last summer's crop. The kids wear hand-me-downs from their siblings and vintage T-shirts scavenged at thrift stores.

The mom washes her hair only once a week and doesn't color it because of the chemicals. (She looks great anyway.) She gets up early every morning to check the garden and read poetry. She doesn't drink soda. The dad plays the harmonica near the wood stove at night, while the kids do their homework on paper they recycled themselves. They don't have a television. This imaginary family is kind and smart and responsible and attractive. Also, they never quibble over who left the closet door open.

As you might guess, this is not what my family looks like.

Our yard is huge, with tons of grass to mow. We don't use a hose or a sprinkler system to keep it irrigated, in part because we believe in water conservation (but also because who has the time for that?). I know how to sew on a button, and that's about it. I can cook well enough to keep us reasonably healthy, but sometimes I really want a Diet Coke and some peanut M&Ms. We drive almost everywhere we go. We use cloth napkins and dish towels instead of paper—but then we spend a lot of energy and water in the washing machine, and when our clothesline fell down a while back, we just never replaced it, and now the hammock is hanging in its place, and we dry almost everything in the electric dryer. We don't watch our TV that often, but that's usually because we're streaming Netflix onto one of our various laptops. (When you live with an IT guy, you accumulate a lot of computer equipment.)

I realize that this is dumb, comparing our real life to some imaginary, idealized version of somebody else's, but

I find myself always looking for an out: nobody really lives like that, right? Barbara Kingsolver's book *Animal, Vegetable, Miracle*, which tells how she and her family committed to eating only locally grown food for a year, was hugely inspirational to me. But still I felt immense relief to find, tucked into her final pages, the admission that sometimes she fed her daughter store-bought mac and cheese.[2] Aha! I thought.

One blog I read regularly is written by a woman whose family is homesteading, living off their land, sewing their own clothes. Even as I'm inspired by her way of life, I find myself on the lookout for times she slips up: They ordered take-out pizza! Her kids wear jeans! Was that a plastic toy I saw in the background of that picture of freshly canned beans?

It's not fair to judge a life — my own or anybody else's — by arbitrary standards, and an actual definition of "the simple life" is hard to pin down. Doris Janzen Longacre, who quite literally wrote the book on simple living more than thirty years ago (more on her in a minute), calls it "living more with less." Some say it's living close to the land, growing your own food, reducing waste, not relying so much on consumer goods. For others, it's limiting the acquisition of new stuff or downsizing the stuff you have. It's being free from possessions and wealth.

For many, the simple life is about sustainability and justice: when we use less, other people have more. But I've also heard people talk about living simply for the sake of their own health and well-being; minimizing the demands of the world, for them, makes for better mental health and decreased stress. Not having to keep up with the Joneses frees them to live their own lives.

Some simple-lifers are into the tiny-house trend. Resourceful, industrious people are creating living spaces out of things like shipping containers or backyard storage sheds, living in houses the size of an oversize closet. Or they're withdrawing from society as much as possible, building their own primitive homes off the grid.

A longtime member of my church died recently, after a long and full life. As we prepared for the funeral, her family told me she lived with a frugality that was characteristic of her generation, which came of age during the Great Depression. Her motto, her kids told me with a laugh, was "Use it up, wear it out, make your own, or do without," which seems about as good a definition as any to describe a life lived simply.

These definitions are all well and good, but the more I search, the more I realize that a "simple life" may not be what I'm after.

The truth is that if living well and faithfully means living simply, then I'm failing every day. A faithful life might include decluttering my house, eating local foods, making my own whatever, or doing without, but that can't be the end of the story. What I want is something other (or something more?) than a simple life. I want to live in a way that acknowledges that life is not simple, at all, and that we can live faithfully in the midst of it anyway.

I'm not so sure that a complicated life is all that bad. That pile of preschool artwork and second-grade homework on my kitchen counter might be clutter, but it's also proof that my kids are being taught by excellent teachers and are thriving under their care. These gadgets that are plugged in all over my house—my phone, my laptop, the TV—are using up electricity, but they're also helping me do a job I love, stay in touch with my faraway family, and enjoy a cheap date night with Rob at the end of a long week. And for now, when produce is plentiful in this part of the country, I'll eat North Carolina strawberries. But come winter, I'm going to be grateful for oranges and bananas, even if they were shipped from a long way away.

Or take last week: Harper started complaining that her throat hurt on Wednesday afternoon, and when she crawled into bed with us early Thursday, I could tell by the touch of her forehead that she had a fever, and I would have bet you my cloth napkins it was strep. The doctor's office scheduled us quickly, and I was right: off we went to the drugstore for antibiotics (the pink yummy stuff this time, thankfully; last time, when the doctor prescribed a different kind, we had to do battle at every meal to get her to take it). So we went to the doctor, then the drugstore, then to pick up lunch (factory-farmed chicken from a drive-through!) and through the ATM at the bank. All of these errands were within a mile of my house, all easily and safely walkable. We could have done without the car.

There's probably no real excuse for the fast-food lunch. And the reality is that I drive to the bank and the drugstore all the time, even though I could walk, because walking takes longer and time is at a premium around here. But last Thursday, my kid had strep throat and a fever and is too young to be left alone. So if she needs antibiotics, she's got to come with me to the store to get them, and really, wouldn't you think less of me for making my poor sick kid walk when we could have taken the car?

See what I mean? Nothing simple about it.

Sometimes the simplest choice is not the choice that connects with the kind of life I want to live or the sort of community I want to live in. It's more simple to order a book online—right now, in my pajamas, at midnight, and the book will be at my house on Friday afternoon—than it is to go to the bookstore that just opened downtown and see if they have it in stock, which they probably don't, and even if they can order it, it'll be next week before I can go back and get it. That's not simple, but I want to live in a community that has a local bookstore, which depends on support from customers like me, which means that I've got to do the more complicated thing. In the end, a "simple life" is not what I'm longing for.

I need to say this, too: there's something significantly different between *choosing* a simple life and having one forced on you. It's one thing for me to walk to the store on a sunny day when I have time; it's an entirely different thing for the woman waiting for the bus in the rain so that she can get to work. The choice to live simply is, in many ways, another by-product of privilege.

This then points to the need for advocacy and changed systems (more on that in chapter 11): Why aren't there more reliable public transportation systems? Why is junk food so cheap? Why can't we figure out a way to make healthy food more affordable and accessible?

Why is it so complicated to let others simply live?

◌◌◌

The move toward simple living may be trendy right now, but it's not new. The Desert Mothers and Fathers were monastics who withdrew from society and lived in the desert of Egypt in the third century. Francis of Assisi took on a life of voluntary poverty in the twelfth century. Gandhi did the same in the early twentieth. Jesus lived pretty simply, too, from what we know about his life (though I doubt he ever agonized about ordering books from the local bookstore).

A number of Christian communities in the United States have advocated for simple living for a long time. Chief among them was the voice of Doris Janzen Longacre, who was writing about, and actually practicing, the simple life long before there were blogs and Internet forums devoted to tiny houses.

I'd been aware of Longacre's book *Living More with Less*, and its companion cookbook, for some time, having walked by it and even skimmed through it in bookstores for years, but I confess to not wanting to actually pick it up, fearful that it would set yet another expectation that I could never live up to. My reluctance to read it was shared by Valerie Weaver-Zercher, who revised and edited Longacre's work for the thirtieth-anniversary edition.

The pattern for more-with-less living that Doris Janzen Longacre outlined in *Living More with Less*, paired with its classification as a home economics volume, looked to me like one more way to make homemakers (still mostly women, still mostly mothers) feel like they weren't doing enough. The time and energy to "green" one's life, as popular parlance had branded it, felt like privileges I didn't have and couldn't summon. So it was that I spent my days caroming between self-righteousness when I met my more-with-less ideals (full laundry line! local foods for dinner!) and self-reproach when I didn't (countless trips in the gas-hogging minivan! frozen pizza!). . . . The 1980 *Living More with Less* sat mutely on my bookshelf, and I avoided cracking its aging spine.[3]

Exactly.

With the assurance that the updated version of the book was slightly gentler, I did crack the spine and start reading. It was true: the book has high expectations for its readers, despite the recognition throughout its pages that it's never as easy as it sounds. The sheer number of ideas and suggestions for "living more with less" is overwhelming and left me feeling like I would never be able to live up to the ideal, nor would I want to.

It hasn't become a mainstay for nothing, though, and I did find Longacre's framework helpful, if not the torrent of things I should do differently in my life. She suggests "Five Life Standards" as a way of shaping our way of life:

Do justice, "being mindful, conscious, and aware, so that never again can we make a decision about buying and using without thinking of the poor."

Learn from the world community, that is, paying attention to the life practices of our global neighbors and considering what we can learn from them.

Nurture people, "[bringing] others to this full life and growth in the kingdom of God."

Cherish the natural order, honoring the earth and all of creation.

Nonconform freely, swimming upstream against the current of culture.[4]

These life standards acknowledge that simple living is about the whole world and not just me, that living well includes caring for creation and our neighbors—with a particular eye to the needs of the poor—as well as ourselves and our own families. These ideas are pretty central to the Christian faith, too (this is no coincidence, of course; Longacre was a faithful Mennonite), which also makes them more compelling to me than the currently trendy call to simple living. The prophets call us to do justice, Jesus welcomes people from all kinds of other cultures and traditions, his final commandment to the disciples is to love one another, we worship God as creator of all that is, and there's no real question that the Christ who died on the cross was a nonconformist.

One of the things I appreciate about Longacre's approach is that her "life standards" are not a list of rules, not a list of dos and don'ts. Rather than, say, forbidding us to buy anything plastic ever, these standards challenge us to ask questions that might help us make a faithful choice. Will buying this plastic thing help us nurture people? What impact will this plastic thing have on the poor or on our earth? Am I buying this plastic thing because that's what everybody else in the culture is doing? How do people in other cultures address the need for whatever it is?

Tsh Oxenreider, whose approach to living simply is far less extreme than that of the tiny-house-off-the-grid advocates and whose blog *The Art of Simple* offers all kinds of encouragement and advice on living the simple life, says that simple living is "living holistically with your life's purpose." That's a decent definition, but it takes a bit of unpacking, since you first have to figure out what your life's purpose is. Actually, I like even more what Oxenreider says about what the simple life is not: "It's not a backwards race to see who can live with the least amount of stuff" or a competition in which our success is judged by somebody else's priorities. Nor is it an end in itself; living simply ought to make your life better or make somebody else's life better. "I believe," she says, "that relationships are more important than things, and that life is so much better when we live beyond ourselves."[5] I can get on board with that.

What Longacre, Oxenreider, and others are proposing — and, ultimately, what I'm in search of—is a way of life, not a list of rules.

ᏯᏄᏯ

I knew that I'd never be the kind of person who makes my own clothes (though I did once make a pair of hot pink parachute pants in eighth-grade home ec class. What? You didn't?), but I thought maybe I could grow some of our own food. I wanted to love gardening; I really did. Shortly after Rob and I got married and moved into a second-floor condo with a little balcony off the back, I took a class at the local rec center on container gardening. I retained very little of that knowledge, though I do now know to pluck off basil down at the V of the plant rather than pull the leaves off individually. It forces the growth back down into the plant and keeps it growing for the rest of the summer.

I took that class about the time I read Kingsolver's book about local foods, and I scouted out the farmers' markets in town. We joined a CSA that summer, too—a community-supported agriculture program, in which you buy a "share" of produce from a nearby farm. Each week, I got acquainted with a new vegetable; I learned to love Swiss chard but never did figure out what to do with turnips.

A few years later, when we moved into a house with a yard, we built a couple of raised garden beds in the sunniest corner. We planted lettuce, green peppers, cucumbers, basil, spinach, several kinds of tomatoes. I was especially excited about the tomatoes — I had visions of thick slices on bread, and small grape tomatoes tossed with pasta. I imagined the surplus I would take over to share with our neighbors.

I made several trips to the garden store for more soil, fertilizer, tomato cages . . . then later went back for chicken wire and bird netting to keep out whatever critters were eating everything.

Let's just say it did not go particularly well. The plants grew—they were tall and full and green; they just didn't produce much fruit. When there was a tiny cucumber or pepper starting to grow, a bird or a squirrel would make off with it, and I'd find it half-eaten in the driveway the next day. Or something—I suspected a stray cat—would eat the plants themselves; one morning I came out to find the tomatoes completely decimated, all the plants broken off at the stem.

Optimistically, we tried this for several seasons in a row, always hoping that the year before had been a fluke, that this would be the season when we'd get it right. Finally, last year, we scaled it back to just a couple of tomato plants, some lettuce, and basil. Those two tomato plants yielded exactly one tiny handful of cherry tomatoes. No juicy slices, not enough for pasta, none worth sharing.

So this year, I gave it up. As it turns out, I'm not very good at growing things. Maybe I just don't know enough or I'm not patient enough or I'm too busy with other things. Whatever the reason, it seems that my thumb is just not that green.

The overgrown beds were taunting me all spring, though, as the yard came back to life from the winter and the kudzu threatened to take over. On Mother's Day weekend, I bought some annual flowers—impatiens, petunias, begonias—in a variety of colors, and the kids and I set out to plant them. We cleared out the weeds and turned the soil. They dug little holes in the garden beds, and I carefully popped the plants out of the containers. Jonathan did the white ones, Harper did the red, patting the dirt back down around the base of the plant.

In the other bed, we planted basil and cilantro. Basil's been the one plant that's always been there for me, ever since that rec center class. It's hardy and forgiving and excellent on pizza. I haven't had as much luck with cilantro, but I couldn't resist the thought of fresh salsa in another month or two.

That's it. No peppers or zucchini. No squash. No blueberries along the back fence. No heirloom tomatoes destined to break my heart. If we remember to water our little flowers and herbs, so be it; if not, we'll just trust the rain to come when we need it. I'm not going to spend any more time agonizing over my little garden.

I can't do my job and keep up with the laundry and toilet train Jonathan and take Harper to swim practice and learn how to grow tomatoes too, I told myself. Maybe in another season of my life I'll be able to grow my own dinner; at the moment, it's all I can do to get it on the table most nights. It's just too complicated.

But then a member of my church—the coordinator of our church garden ministry and an excellent gardener himself—got wind of my forfeit and decided that perhaps my thumb could be turned green with a little encouragement. (If you don't have some church people in your life, remedy that; they're the best.)

I may not be great at growing things. I am, however, reasonably capable of receiving gifts, especially in the form of a giant, already-flowering, abundantly healthy cherry tomato plant, dropped off on my front porch. He had pulled a volunteer plant up from the ground where it had sprouted from seeds dropped by last year's fruits, potted it in rich soil, put a tomato cage around it, and then wrapped the whole thing in netting to keep out the critters. "I'll drop it off tomorrow," he said when he called. "All you have to do is keep it watered."

So far, so good. A few are ripe today, and if I'm not mistaken, we'll be swimming in cherry tomatoes this time next week. I'm not sure which I appreciate more: the tomatoes themselves, the encouragement to keep trying, or the reminder that we're all in this together, each doing what we know how to do and sharing the fruits of our labors.

I still think it's OK to not do it all or to make a different choice. Buying tomatoes from the farmer at the market who knows how to grow them would have certainly been fine, and I'll still do plenty of that this summer. But also — whether we're talking about local foods or walking to the store or paying attention to where our clothes are made — I think we've got to push ourselves a little bit. We have to do some things differently even if it's hard. We don't have to do it alone. If we're paying attention, we'll see that we've got people around us who know what they're doing, who won't let us off the hook when we give in to the temptation to not even really try, who share what they know and what they have.

That's the power of community right there. We need the ancient witness of the desert monastics and modern-day prophets like Doris Janzen Longacre and Barbara Kingsolver. We need church people who will challenge us, and we need neighbors we can learn from. We need to pay attention to the impact our lives have on the earth and the people around us. We need to do better, and we need to give ourselves and everybody else a little grace.

It might just be that simple after all.

CHAPTER 4

LAMENT

For a brief time a while back, I had a therapist who liked to talk more than she liked to listen. As I like to listen more than I like to talk, this made for an odd and not, finally, compatible patient-therapist relationship. She was perfectly nice, and I learned a lot about her son's graduate school studies, but I didn't find the experience all that helpful to me, which was sort of the point.

In her defense, she did introduce me to the writings of Thich Nhat Hanh and the whole idea of being mindful, which I mostly, sort of, buy. So there was that.

One day, in a rare moment when I got to tell her something about my life, I was trying to articulate how I was feeling about the fate of the world in general. I can't remember now what particular crisis was happening at the moment—I think it was a natural disaster that had killed thousands of people somewhere around the world, the sort of situation made worse by poverty and lack of resources (how glib I sound, protected by the privilege of forgetting most of the world's disasters!)—and I said something about how it was weighing on me.

"Well, can you do anything about that right now?" she countered. I agreed that I probably could not.

So, she said, "Let it go." (She said this without breaking into song, as the movie *Frozen* was still several years away from ruining that phrase for all time.) "You don't have to worry about that one anymore."

"But . . . ," I started to argue.

"Nope—just let it go," she said. I acquiesced, and she launched into a story about her family camping trip.

I see her point. There's no sense worrying about something you can't do anything about. But that's mostly good advice for things like tomorrow's weather forecast.

The truth is, there probably is something we can do about the thorny problems of inequality and injustice.

Even when there really isn't anything to be done, or when our response seems like spitting into the ocean, or when the situation is so thickly complicated that we don't even know where to start—for those times, there is the book of Psalms.

The Psalms—the ancient prayer book of the Scriptures— is smack-dab in the middle of the Bible. It's a trick I still use when presenting Bibles to third-graders at church each fall: I have the kids hold their Bibles up and then open them directly to the center pages and find the Psalms, which is a pretty good place to start.

These ancient poems and songs contain the entirety of human life—joy and sorrow, celebration and grief, confession, praise, gratitude, despair. They remember God's saving acts of power, rejoice in the goodness of God's creation, call on the people to worship and give thanks. They give voice to pain, loneliness, and fear, and they cry out for help.

The psalms of lament—poems that express the darkness of grief or despair, scattered throughout the Psalter—are the hardest to read, sometimes, but they can also be the most real and relevant.

Sometimes they're spoken in the voices of individuals:

> How long must I bear pain in my soul,
>   and have sorrow in my heart all day long?
>
> —Ps. 13:2

I think of people I've known who have cancer—or more often, the spouses, children, and parents of people with cancer. I've heard them lift up prayers of lament like that, when it feels as if there is no way up, no way out of the grief, and the only thing left is to name it and offer it up to God.

Sometimes the laments of the Psalms are communal. They are the voice of a whole people who have lost their way, who fear that God has abandoned them.

> You have made us like sheep for slaughter,
>   and have scattered us among the nations.
> . . . .
>   Why do you forget our affliction and oppression?
> For we sink down to the dust;
>   our bodies cling to the ground.
> Rise up, come to our help.
>
> —Ps. 44:11, 24b–26

The writers of the lament psalms sound sometimes like they have abandoned all faith in God, as they fear God has left them: *My God, my God, why have you forsaken me?*—the lament of Psalm 22, whispered from Jesus' own lips on the cross.

Why have you forsaken us?

And yet, the singers of these sad songs, those who pray these despairing prayers, still cry out to God for help. Therein lies their greatest gift to us, when we lift our own laments, because these psalms betray the deepest possible faith: that only God can save us.

A Psalm of Lament

We remember, O God, the stories of our ancestors,
of how you promised a land of milk and honey,
an abundant life
filled with many good things.

Well, here we are.
Everything we could possibly want.

We are grateful, but we're drowning in this promised land.

Our closets and toy boxes and bookshelves are
    overflowing.

As much as we try to stem the tide
of plastic stuff
as much as we try to resist the urge to
accumulate more -

It keeps coming in.

We're killing this sweet planet of yours.
There are major storms once a week now:
snow
rain
tornado
earthquake
hurricane
typhoon
monsoon

80 degrees one day and 30 the next

The earth is crying out: how long, O Lord, how long?

In the grocery store this morning
as I did my weekly shopping
watching the sales but always picking up something extra
    we could do without
never worried about how I'll feed my family
an employee in the produce section was putting bananas
    in a box.

At first I thought he was just moving them to another
    shelf
but then I watched him squash them down to fit as many
    as he could
a giant pile of smashed bananas

and I realized he was throwing them away
that they were bruised and brown
not even good enough for the discount bin.

Not even worth 10 bananas for a dollar.

Bananas shipped all the way here from banana-growing
    countries
harvested by workers not paid enough because we like
    our bananas cheap
only to end up smashed in a box on the grocery store floor.

They would have been fine in a smoothie
or some banana bread

or, if you just weren't too picky about bananas.

And in the car, NPR is holding a pledge drive
asking for money to fund the radio station
and every pledge, they interrupt the program to
    tell me,
triggers a donation of a backpack filled with food

for a school child who doesn't have anything to eat at
   home on the weekend.

Hurry, God, come and save us.

Here in the promised land
we are starving ourselves to death.

CHAPTER 5

―――――――――――― ∽∽ ――――――――――――

THE VIEW FROM THE
SYCAMORE TREE

*A Rich Man, a Short Man,
and Much Ado about Money*

Lately, Rob and I seem to be failing at some of the basic tasks of being grown-ups. We are generally pretty responsible people, and yet there are days when I wonder if there's anything other than our age that qualifies us to be adults. The grass needs to be mowed, and there are ants in the kitchen that are apparently impervious to any kind of defense against them. We're late getting our tax return together. We can't find any stamps. We're out of checks.

We've been out of checks for some time, actually. We don't use them all that often, as we've got most of our bills set up through the online system at our bank, so we're often scrambling for one when we have to send in money for a field trip or pay a babysitter. For a while I had some in my desk at work, but those are long gone, and the stash that sometimes lived in the pocket of Rob's black jacket seems to be depleted as well. We have none.

Once we discovered they were actually gone, Rob went online and ordered some, which were supposed to take two weeks to arrive. It's been two and a half weeks, we finally calculate — slightly desperate now, because the taxes are due Tuesday and Rob needs to get his passport renewed, which requires a picture, various completed forms, and, of course, a check. So I call the bank, punch through endless menus and finally talk to someone who tells me that the checks have indeed been ordered and shipped and should be arriving any day, but that if I really need some, I can go to my local branch and they can print some temporary checks.

This is relatively helpful advice, so I stop in at the branch on my way to pick up the kids. I haven't been inside the bank in months, maybe a year. We bank at a Big Giant Bank and do almost all our banking online or at the ATM; we both have direct deposit for our paychecks, and lately Rob's even been depositing other checks with his phone. (It's amazing, this world we live in.) We've been talking about switching to a smaller, local bank. Putting our money to work in the community where we live seems like a good idea, and the big banks haven't exactly been the good guys in the economic drama of the last few years. But we haven't done it yet.

At the counter, I explain the situation to the teller — we're out of checks, the new ones haven't arrived — and she tells me she can print some new checks for a dollar each.

I balk. A dollar each! Granted, I only need a few, and I can spare three dollars. But I don't want to spend three dollars when we've been waiting for two and a half weeks for checks we already paid for. I hesitate and make my exasperated-annoyed face (I have a really good exasperated-annoyed face), and the teller calls over her manager, who glances at her screen and then invites me into his office.

I don't really want to go to his office; I just want some checks, and I want to go pick up my kids. But I'm in this far, so I follow him. Judging by his face, I think he's probably younger than me, but he's dressed impeccably in a dark blue business suit and he's very tall. I'm in my yoga pants and a fleece vest, and I haven't washed my hair since yesterday morning. It's silly to be intimidated by him, but I am.

He invites me to sit down and then pecks away at his keyboard. "Let's see what's going on with those checks," he says, looking at the screen. "OK," he says, "they've been reordered, but it'll probably take another couple weeks before they arrive."

I sigh.

"So we'll get you some printed today," he says.

"For a dollar each?" I give him a look.

"Nah, we'll waive that. It's OK."

"Thank you." I'm ready to go, then, and I start to stand up—let's get the checks, get the kids, and go home and finish the taxes—but he's not done.

"I see here that you're eligible for our premium checking account. I can get you set up with that today, if you'd like."

I sit back down. I knew there would be a catch.

"It offers several benefits and doesn't cost anything."

Say no thanks, I think. Say, we're doing just fine with the checking account we have, but thank you for the checks and I'll just be on my way.

"Um . . ." is what I actually say, which he considers an invitation to list the various benefits of said account.

"Well, I'm kind of in a hurry," I finally get in.

"I'll get all the paperwork together and send it to you; you can just sign it and send it back in whenever it's convenient."

"OK," I say, defeated, because it's faster than explaining why I don't really want any more paperwork in my life.

He grins, victorious, and we go back to the teller, who prints a sheet of three checks — it prints crooked but I don't say anything — and I'm finally on my way.

The paperwork arrives the next day in a FedEx over-night envelope (why couldn't the checks have arrived so quickly?) with a prepaid overnight envelope in which to return it. This strikes me as ridiculous: the bank is half a mile from our house; I'll have to go farther away to find a FedEx drop-off spot. Later in the week, a new debit card arrives, followed by a PIN number. Then we realize that Rob's name isn't on the account, and when I call to ask about it, my friendly bank manager tells me that both of us need to come in together to add his name.

A month later, the paperwork—and the overnight envelope—are still sitting on the table, waiting to be dealt with. I'd go ahead and cancel the account, but now that seems as complicated as setting it up.

This is a lot of hassle for a checking account I didn't even want, at a bank I'm not even sure we should be doing business with.

∞∽∞

There's no way around the fact that money plays a central role in our lives. Nathan Dungan, the founder of an organization called Share Save Spend, the mission of which is to help people think more intentionally about the choices they make with their money, says that this is pretty much inevitable.[1] Using money, he says, is like breathing. We all do it, all the time, whether we're aware of it or not. Just by being alive in the world, we all breathe air, and like it or not, we all use money, we buy groceries or pay bills, we pay taxes, we get paid for our work. . . . We can no more avoid interacting with money than we can stop breathing; we just can't do it.

This is not a criticism; this is the way the world works. And it's not new. Through all of history, people have been dealing with money; from barter systems and gift econo-mies to printed currencies to online deposits, there have always been ways that we mark our financial transactions with one another.

But—as in a yoga class when the instructor invites you to focus on the inhale and exhale—it makes a big difference when we pay attention to how we're doing it.

The Bible has plenty to say about money (way more, I'll note, than it says about sex or gay marriage or worship music or any of the things Christians seem to fight about most), but the story that first comes to mind is that of the rich young ruler in Luke 18:18–30 (and also in Matthew and Mark; all three Synoptic Gospel writers thought this was an important story).

A young man comes to Jesus wanting to know how to inherit eternal life—he's heard about Jesus and wants to get in on the action. He assures Jesus that he's a good, upstanding citizen, a rule follower who has obeyed all the commandments since he was a kid. He's done everything right, but still, he's in search of something. He can tell that his life's not right. So Jesus says to him, "Just this one more thing. There's the matter of all your stuff. Sell it and give the money to the poor."

The rich man doesn't like this idea one bit, because he has a lot of stuff; parting with it would be a monumental, life-changing task. Which, of course, is exactly what Jesus intends.

But the man can't do it. He goes away sad and discouraged, still trapped by his possessions, unable to imagine a life that's not built around his riches.

Money does that to people—it's not just that guy, and it doesn't really matter how we define "rich." If we let it, money clouds our vision and chokes up our airways until we can't breathe or see straight.

Recent studies have revealed a growing body of evidence that the wealthier people are, the more likely they are to cheat, take what isn't theirs, or just generally be obnoxious. Financial journalist Michael Lewis writes,

It is beginning to seem that the problem isn't that the kind of people who wind up on the pleasant side of inequality suffer from some moral disability that gives them a market edge. The problem is caused by the inequality itself: It triggers a chemical reaction in the privileged few. It tilts their brains. It causes them to be less likely to care about anyone but themselves or to experience the moral sentiments needed to be a decent citizen.[2]

This ought to be a wake-up call for those of us living in relative comfort. Could we imagine a life not built around our riches?

A few verses after the rich young man walks away from Jesus disappointed, Luke tells us about another rich man named Zacchaeus, who climbs up into a sycamore tree and gives us a different view.

You probably remember Zacchaeus from that children's song; he is most well known for being vertically challenged, "a wee little man was he." That's why he climbed up into the tree to watch for Jesus coming into town. But what that kids' song doesn't emphasize is that Zacchaeus was also pretty rich. Maybe not as rich as the young man in the earlier story, but rich nonetheless. He was a tax collector, which, in those days, meant he was a member of the elite class, had a good job, and quite likely used his position to exploit people and make his own riches even greater. Zacchaeus is another rich man who is interested in what Jesus has to say to him about his life.

We know the story: he climbs into the tree, he sees Jesus coming, and when Jesus sees him up there, he says, let's go have dinner at your house and let's talk a little bit. What's worth paying attention to here is what Zacchaeus does after he comes down from the tree, after he has dinner with Jesus.[3]

He gives away half of what he has.

He promises to make things right with anybody he'd cheated.

He finds salvation.

And right there, I think Zacchaeus gives us another—maybe more workable—model for how to live faithfully with what we have. Listen:

He gives away half. Not all. But a significant percentage. Without a doubt, he still has enough to live on, comfortably, enough to enjoy life. But he gives generously, significantly.

He makes things right with anybody he's cheated. He makes amends and vows to stop doing business the way he'd been doing it.

And Jesus says, "Today salvation has come to this house." Going forward, Zacchaeus is going to live a different life. And while that's the last we hear of him, I like to think that Zacchaeus was changed that day. I like to think that the view from the sycamore tree changed his mind about how he was living and that going forward, he would make sure that nobody else got hurt in the process.

That seems like a pretty good model:

Give generously, make amends, do as little harm as possible.

That's awfully different from the life he was living before.

Are we going to live the way we've always lived? Or can we imagine a new way of life?

The first rich young man couldn't imagine a new way, but Zacchaeus could. Maybe because he climbed that tree and the view was clearer up there. Perhaps that's what we need, too: a new vantage point, a new way of seeing. We need to imagine a new relationship with our money.

Let's take a look at Zacchaeus's new model for living with money and see if it might offer a way ahead: Give generously, make amends, and do as little harm as possible going forward.

Now, I'm going to assume that you are a person who is generally inclined toward generosity, that you already understand how important giving is. My dad, who is himself a very generous and financially savvy person, says that one of the reasons that giving is good for you—in addition to the good work that gets done with the gifts—is that it puts you in charge. If you're making a commitment to give away a certain amount of money every month/week/year, then you are controlling your money instead of your money controlling you.

When I think about my own giving practices, one of the things that inspires me is the realization that everything I've ever done has been funded by other people's generosity. The majority of my education and every job and internship I've ever had—with the exception of two summers working in the Kmart electronics department (fun fact!)—has been made possible by donations from people who thought that work was important. That's not true for everybody, of course, but even for people who haven't spent their lives working for churches and nonprofits, it's worth remembering that whatever money we have—just like all our possessions—isn't really ours. It's passing through our hands for a while, and we had better put it to good use.

I wish it were as simple as that. I wish that solving the world's injustices were as easy as giving away some money. But the reality is that sometimes our money has caused more problems than it has solved. And though I don't think I've ever been as intentionally corrupt as Zacchaeus probably was, I know that just by participating in the economy, I've had a negative impact on the world.

I have never studied economics, but I did have the good fortune of having lunch not too long ago with my friend Rebecca Todd Peters. She's a professor of religion and ethics and has written widely about global economics. She says that you have to understand some history to understand the structures of our current global economy. She writes,

The allure of an ideology that recognizes the capitalist, consumerist, and individualistic way of life as the pinnacle of civilization, and a capitalist market economy as superior to all others, has structured our lives in particular ways. Unfortunately, privilege and wealth are too often accompanied by a complacency that blinds us to our own weakness. As a country, we have become a people that are largely ignorant of the economic institutions of globalization like the IMF, World Bank, or WTO. Many people in the United States do not know what these institutions do or how they function, but ignorance does not reduce the moral culpability of US Americans for the actions of their government working through these institutions.[4]

Guilty. I have only a vague idea of what the IMF, World Bank, and WTO do, and an even vaguer idea of what that has to do with me.

Here's a quick primer if you're in the same boat: The International Monetary Fund (IMF) and the World Bank were formed in the aftermath of World War II in an effort to help with postwar reconstruction and keep the world from sinking into the sort of Great Depression that had rocked the United States in the 1930s. The World Trade Organization (WTO), though not officially formed until 1995, was an outgrowth of that same international postwar movement. The IMF and the WTO work to ensure the stability of international financial markets, with a goal of expanding growth and increasing international trade. The World Bank's stated goal is to alleviate global poverty by providing loans and grants to developing countries.

That all sounds good, but Peters (among others) points out that these organizations were formed by and continue to exist for an economic system in which the rich get richer and the poor get poorer. The problem is that those financial institutions have adopted a one-size-fits-all approach to global development, without giving much say to the countries who are supposedly being helped. Peters says that we really ought to be asking, "What effect do these policies have on the poor and the most marginalized people in society?"⁴

That's a little like what Zacchaeus found himself thinking about when Jesus came over for dinner; maybe that's the question that moved him to make amends, to pay back the people he cheated. And if that's the model we're following, how can we do the same?

I'm not sure I'll ever get my head around those big global institutions, but I can learn more and pay better attention to what they're doing. And I can support organizations that are working for real systemic change and not just putting Band-Aids on problems. That way, even though my money has been the cause of growing inequalities, maybe it will also be part of the solution.

Others are imagining new ways of relating to our money, too, often in ways that attempt to lessen existing injustices. Micro credit loans are one way I see this happening. Through organizations like Kiva or Oikocredit, low-income entrepreneurs around the world can receive small loans to support their local businesses. The loans are paid back, so it's not charity—but the loans don't earn interest and many investors just reinvest the funds in another project, so it's not exactly a moneymaking venture either. It's not perfect, but it's a model that works around traditional banking systems and gives us a new vantage point on our relationship with money.

After talking about it for the better part of a year, Rob and I finally opened a new checking account at a smaller local bank. Inertia's the only reason I can suggest to explain why it took us so long. We knew we wanted to, and the bank's right up the street—in the same shopping center as the old bank, so it's no less convenient. After a few bumps at the beginning, it hasn't been all that much different.

I'm trusting that what they say is true, that local banks are better for the community, that the people who make the decisions live here in town and are more likely to keep the community in mind, that the customer service is better, that the bank will invest more in local people and businesses.

We've still got a ways to go. Our mortgage is still at the Big Giant Bank, and we've got some investments doing who knows what in mutual funds that are nearly impossible to track down. We've looked into socially responsible investing—I even bought a book, *Socially Responsible Investing for Dummies*, but it, too, is a minefield of complications. It sounds like it should be simple: you invest your money in companies whose values you support. But unless you know enough to actually do the investing yourself, you're going to have to trust a fund manager whose values might be different from your own. Plus, there's that whole inertia thing.

So right now we're living in the imperfect place of doing what we can and knowing we could do better.

∞∞

In addition to evaluating our own money practices, I also want to think carefully about how we talk about money with our kids. I don't suppose I'll be explaining the World Bank to Harper anytime soon, but we can make sure that money isn't a taboo topic around our house.

When I asked Nathan Dungan for some advice about talking with kids about money, he told me about a game he plays with his own four-year-old daughter. He shows her coins: a quarter, a nickel, a penny. If she can name it and tell him how much it's worth, she gets to keep it. The money she keeps then gets evenly divided into the three compartments of her share/save/spend bank. "As parents," he says, "it's our role to shape our kids' money narrative." If we don't, the culture around us will.

Dungan advocates against using popular electronic allowance tracking systems, widely available online or as smartphone apps. Kids like to feel money; cash and coins are tangible items they can touch with their hands and put somewhere. For children, touching is a big part of the learning experience, and virtual allowances take that away. Kids need practice, and using real money helps. Plus, there's evidence that adults spend less when they use cash than when they use intangible credit; helping kids deal with cash instills good money habits early on.

Dungan says he also talks with his daughter about their family's money choices. He describes taking her to the farmers' market, biking to work, living in the city with one car. His daughter doesn't watch commercial TV, and they avoid clothes with characters on them or toys that promote something else. But he's quick to point out that perfection isn't the goal and that each family needs to identify their own values and habits—which reminds me of Longacre's five life standards for simple living: it's not a list of rules, but a way of life.

One of the resources developed by Share Save Spend is a series of "Money Talk" questions, discussion starters designed to get parents and kids talking. Harper picks it up from the kitchen table one day and asks if we can "play." It's not really a game, but she's interested enough that we spend quite a bit of time asking each other questions. Some go over her head—it's more geared toward older kids and teens—but some are right on: *What things do you have of which you can't have just one?* We talk about her bracelet loom, which needs refills, and her toy ponies, which have endless accessories, all sold separately. One question gives her pause: *Should adults expect kids to share some of their money?* At first she says no, but I finally realize she's thinking of the kind of sharing we make her do with her brother. When I suggest sharing some money with people who don't have enough food, she's on board. These are good conversations to have, and I can see how it's a lot easier to start talking now, when it's toy ponies at stake, rather than in a few years when we're talking about cars and college tuition.

Shortly after I talk with Dungan, I'm at the pool with my kids, fielding the now-regular needling for a snack from the concession stand. "Please, Mom? Some chips?"

I tell her no, again, and she sighs, heading off to find her friend. When I catch up with her a minute later, I realize why she'd been so insistent: her friend is on her way to the concession stand, an envelope marked "spend" in hand. "By any chance," I ask her, "do you have a 'share' and a 'save' envelope at home?" She nods, and I resolve to come up with a similar system for my daughter. It occurs to me that Dungan's right: we need to give our kids a chance to practice dealing with money. They'll be doing it all their lives—it's like breathing, after all—and we want them to do it well.

CHAPTER 6

―――――― ⟨◌⟩⟨◌⟩ ――――――

CONFESSION

Last summer, Rob and I took off for a grown-ups–only vacation to Barcelona, thanks to grandparents who stayed with the kids and some intentional saving we did over the past few years. In between stops for tapas, we walked and walked through the narrow brick streets of the city's oldest neighborhoods, marveling at the history built into the very walls, while modern urban life bustled right on around it. Every few blocks, it seemed, we came across a church: a tall cathedral or old basilica or just a neighborhood sanctuary. Most were open to the public, so we often stepped in to look around, the quiet, ancient dark a sharp contrast to the loud and sunny streets outside.

We were never the only tourists, but even among the cameras and the backpacks, there was a reverence to the sacred space. Tall vaulted ceilings, heavy wooden doors built into thick stone walls, tables full of small white votives in deep red candleholders, lit by the faithful who lifted up their prayers. In one such church, I was struck by the beauty of an old confessional booth, built from beautifully carved dark wood. It would have looked so out of place in my Protestant, 1950s-era church back home, but tucked in the corner of this centuries-old worship place, it was just right. I stood in front of it for a moment, imagining the generations of people who had slipped into the booth to whisper their confessions to the priest on the other side.

❦

Confession: In the middle of writing about simple living, I stop for lunch: a frozen pizza and a Diet Coke. I glance at the ingredients on the soda bottle: not a bit of actual nutrients or real food. The pizza can't be much better; I don't even want to look. But it is quick and easy, and comfort food. I eat it all.

Confession: Halloween is tonight. I've read the articles about chocolate and the child slave trade, and I am blatantly ignoring the problem. I bought a huge bag of Tootsie Rolls, and I fully intend to sneak the good candy bars out of my kids' bags after they go to bed.

Confession: "The desire to do good is inside of me, but I can't do it. I don't do the good that I want to do, but I do the evil that I don't want to do" (Rom. 7:18b–19 CEB).

❦

In one conversation I had about the question of living faithfully when we have more than others in the world, one woman's response has stuck with me. She was a lawyer and had what was apparently a relatively lucrative career. She was in her late 40s, probably, or maybe early 50s.

"Believe me," she said, more than once, "it makes me really uncomfortable to know that I don't have to struggle to pay the bills." She repeated this conviction several times, voicing it in so many different ways that I began to think that she was pretty comfortable in her discomfort and was content to stay there.

I've pondered that since, because I wonder if that's true of me. Perhaps I am not all that interested in changing anything about my life; I just want to let people know how concerned I am about it.

Confession: I like my comfortable life.

A group of folks at my church right now are learning about Ignatian spirituality, an approach to the life of faith practiced by the Jesuit religious community founded by Ignatius of Loyola. One of the prayer practices that Ignatius made popular is called the examen. When you do the daily practice of examen, you think back over the past twenty-four hours, notice the moments when you most felt God's presence, and give thanks for the things for which you are grateful. Then, still thinking back over the past day, you acknowledge the things you did that you shouldn't have or the things you didn't do that you should have, hand those things over to God, and receive God's grace.

Put simply, in the midst of all the gratitude, you offer up your confession.

Confession is an important part of our tradition that we sometimes overlook, or we dismiss it as something outdated and quaint. Some Christian traditions still use confessional booths like the one I saw in Barcelona. Others — especially of the more Protestant variety — encourage individual and communal confession through spoken or silent prayers in the weekly worship service. Still others rarely give voice to confessional prayers at all except in particular church seasons like Lent. But this ancient practice could be vital to freeing us, and the world, from the grip of whatever it is that holds us captive.

Because the truth is, sometimes we have something to confess. Sometimes we're guilty.

Now, "guilt" is a loaded word, I know. There are different types of guilt, which is to say, there are different types of sin, and sin, as you probably know, can be awfully hard to define. (Barbara Brown Taylor's book *Speaking of Sin* is a good place to start if you want to think more about this.)[1]

The best definition of sin I've ever heard was shared with me several years ago at a Bible study I was leading. The group was wrestling with how we define sin, and we'd listed all the traditional definitions: missing the mark, rebellion, separation from God. One participant had been quiet throughout the conversation and then finally spoke up. "Here's how I see it," he said. "Sin happens any time the flow of love gets interrupted." He grabbed a marker and drew a big circle on the pad of newsprint at the front of the room. "Like this," he said, and wrote the words "God," "self," and "other people" around the edges of the circle.

"This is the flow of love," he said, drawing arrows pointing to and from each word around the circle. "And anytime it gets interrupted"—here, he drew a thick, dark line intersecting the arrows at each point—"that's sin." Abuse or infidelity in a relationship interrupts the flow of love between people. Not tending to our spiritual lives or neglecting the needs of our bodies interrupts the flow of love from God to us.

The tough thing about sin, though, is that sometimes it's not entirely clear when we're guilty of interrupting that flow of love, especially in the everyday life choices we make all the time. Is it sinful to drive to the store when I could take the car? Is signing up with a local bank less sinful than sticking with our Big Giant Bank? It'd be easier if sins could be listed clearly in a set of rules, like the dos and don'ts camp counselors give on the first day of camp. Don't sneak out of your cabin after lights out; don't go swimming unless the lifeguard is there.

It would be easier if we knew when we were breaking the rules.

And what about the things we didn't mean to do? What about the things we couldn't help doing? Then we feel bad about something we're not sure we really did and wouldn't necessarily have known how to do differently.

It gets tricky when the guilt isn't easily traced back to a particular action of mine. We're all a part of this big system, so unless I've removed myself completely—unlikely and unrealistic—chances are good that I did do something that made somebody else's life a little worse off. I know I'm complicit in the brokenness of the world, the economic systems that benefit the first world at the expense of the rest . . . but what am I supposed to do with that particular guilt?

What about the guilt that is not about something we did or didn't do, but instead is simply because we live at a certain place and a certain time? Ought we feel guilty for simply being born into a system that shows favor to us in unjust proportions?

Maybe I should speak for myself here. I started life with a whole bunch of advantages that I didn't have anything to do with: the education of my parents, the color of my skin, my geographic location on the globe, the genes in my family that seem minimally predisposed to disease or addiction. All those things have made my life easier and have played a pretty big part in making my life as comfortable as it is. I've worked hard, too, but the reality is that I started at a different place than a lot of people.

That's what we call privilege, and sometimes that gets all wrapped up with guilt.

To which writer James Baldwin says this:

I'm not interested in anybody's guilt. Guilt is a luxury that we can no longer afford. I know you didn't do it, and I didn't do it either, but I am responsible for it because I am a man and a citizen of this country and you are responsible for it, too, for the very same reason."[2]

Fair enough. Guilt doesn't do any good if it just swirls around the pit of one's stomach and makes us feel bad. Just as choice is a luxury of the privileged, so is the very fact that I'm fretting about all this in the first place. Which is not to say that I ought not fret, but that fretting gets us nowhere. Guilt is only helpful if we name it (that's what confession is all about), let go of it (that's where grace comes in), and resolve to do better.

And so we confess our sins.

⁂

Confession is a way of telling the truth about our lives. The truth is that we are human and prone to sin. The truth is that sometimes we take more than our share. The truth is that sometimes we can't help but participate in an unjust system. The truth is that sometimes we're the reason that the flow of love between God and the world gets interrupted. The truth is that we live in a broken world that very much needs God's grace.

The Book of Common Prayer puts it this way:

> Most merciful God,
> we confess that we have sinned against you
> in thought, word, and deed,
> by what we have done,
> and by what we have left undone.
> We have not loved you with our whole heart;
> we have not loved our neighbors as ourselves.
> We are truly sorry and we humbly repent.
> For the sake of your Son Jesus Christ,
> have mercy on us and forgive us;
> that we may delight in your will,

and walk in your ways,
to the glory of your Name.
Amen.[3]

Guilt is real, and we ought to pay attention to it—that's why I like that practice of the examen so much; it makes us pay attention—but guilt is never the end of the story. Only when we name our sin can we move past guilt and receive God's grace.

"As hard as such a confession may be," Barbara Brown Taylor writes, "it is also a confession of hope—that things may change, that the way they are is not the way they must always be. The catch, of course, is that this hope begins with some acceptance of your responsibility for the way things are."[4] We make our confession before God, then, but also, sometimes, before our neighbors, whom we have not loved as fully as we ought, whom we have harmed even without intent, by things done and left undone. We have sinned.

Confession matters. Whether whispered in the dim light of an ancient confessional or spoken aloud in a modern sanctuary or prayed at night as we slip off to sleep, confession names our sin and moves us past guilt and into grace—where, finally, we are free to live a different way. Grace is freedom, ultimately, from all that holds us captive: anxiety, scarcity, money, possessions, fear. Grace frees us to participate in what God is doing here, creating and re-creating a redeemed world.

For by grace you have been saved through faith, and this is not your own doing; it is the gift of God (Eph. 2:8).

CHAPTER 7

⸻ ∽◯∽ ⸻

BLESSING AND CURSE

What's with All This Stuff?

I feel about Costco the same way I feel about our minivan: as soon as we had a second kid and bought a house, there was a certain inevitability to it. *Of course* we will have a van, and *of course* we will shop at Costco, with its very crowded parking lot and oversized everything.

In mid-November, we finally gave in and bought a membership. Rob actually went in to fill out the paperwork, which left me on my own for my first excursion. I'm the primary grocery shopper in our family, which I'm generally OK with, so it fell to me to take on the Costco run as well. (I'm learning that you don't "just run into Costco" to pick up anything. It's a serious investment of time. No wonder they sell hot dogs.)

Before going, I mentioned our new membership in a Facebook post and asked for advice. I was unprepared for the passion my friends clearly have for all things Costco. Lasagna! they said. Cheese! Socks! Eyeglasses! Fruit! "The big bag of frozen blueberries changed our lives," one friend commented, and I'm pretty sure he was serious.

The first time I went—which also, regrettably, happened to be the weekend before Thanksgiving—I nearly turned around and walked out, so big and crowded and overwhelming it all seemed. I do like a good deal, though, so I persevered, pushing the giant cart through the towering shelves, wandering past multipacks of Q-tips and boxed chocolates, the famed socks, a child's bike, and giant bags of shredded cheese, in search of the toilet paper aisle. (Would a sign or two hurt? I wondered.)

It's like its own little world in there. Except, not little. Big. Everything is big. The parking lot is big. The doors are big. The carts are big. The shelves are big. The freezer compartments are big. I reached into one of them, trying to reach a boxed pizza near the back of the shelf, and found myself leaning in all the way to my waist. I had visions of falling in and never being heard from again.

The possibilities of this place are endless: I can stock up on vegetables, pick out some new underwear, have a piece of pizza and maybe a churro, buy a new cell phone, sign up for life insurance, and get new tires, all while pushing a cart the size of a small car.

By the time I found the toilet paper and a case of baby wipes (we're almost out of the diapers stage by now, but my sister and her kids were coming to visit, and I figured we could always use wipes for messy hands . . . right? Or are my kids going to inherit all these wipes when I die?), I'd had all I could take, and I pushed my way toward the checkout line, where all the other giant carts were stocked with other giant purchases.

On the way out to the car, I couldn't shake the feeling that there's something slightly (maybe more than slightly) troubling about this place and our love of all things big. Even if it is a good deal, even if we'll use it up eventually, even if it won't go to waste, what does it do to our psyche to default to supersize?

We Americans are pretty comfortable with big. It's practically in our DNA, with the whole Manifest Destiny thing. From the beginning of our story (at least, the story of the European Americans who colonized the "New World"; calling that the beginning is problematic in itself), we've told ourselves that we're entitled to all the land we could get our hands on, regardless of whether anybody was already there. We've never quite shaken that hunger for more. We want it all; we want it all *now*. It's a hard narrative to resist. Why buy one regular-sized bottle of shampoo when you could buy three gallon-sized containers? Why buy enough food for this week when you could buy enough for the whole month? Why not gather in as much as our carts and minivans and garages can hold? Why not take as much as we can get?

If this sounds familiar, it's the same thing that was happening that night at the sledding hill, when we all wanted to hang on to our sleds. It's straight out of the narrative of scarcity that Walter Brueggemann uses to talk about the Hebrew slaves in Egypt, who were part of an economy that required more of everything all the time. Only when God frees them and graces them with the gift of manna in the wilderness do they begin to understand what it means to be free. And it's no coincidence that you can't get manna at Costco; you can only gather it up a day's worth at a time. No buying it in bulk and storing it up for later.

Only when we begin to trust in God's abundance will we be free to know that we will have enough.

Just about every conversation I have with other parents turns at some point to the topic of how much material stuff you accumulate when you have kids. Even when we put limits on it, even when we purge the toy bin every few months, the stuff keeps coming in. Just yesterday Harper came home from the dentist with a small green plastic monkey, a prize from the treasure box for sitting still for her cleaning. It's no big deal, that little monkey, but I'm pretty sure that it will either break or be lost in the next two days, resulting in dramatic tears, or that I will be picking it up off the floor for the next six months.

It's true that nature abhors a vacuum and that any clean surface gets cluttered up as soon as I turn my back. We moved to North Carolina from Washington, DC, a few years ago, a move that included a significant change in housing prices. All our stuff, which had previously filled a tiny two-bedroom condo, magically expanded to fill a two-story house, a shed, and a garage. Where did it all come from?

The reality is that life just comes with stuff. We can bemoan this fact and do our best to keep the tidal wave from swamping us, but we would be foolish to say that our stuff is not important. The material goods that make up our lives — our shoes, toys, chairs, spoons, computers, cars, books, bicycles — have meaning and usefulness. Our stuff keeps us clothed and connected and fed. It helps us create and do good work. Our stuff enhances our lives, makes us happy, helps us learn and grow. I think of the Legos that Jonathan is obsessed with right now. I get awfully tired of cleaning them up, but those bricks have helped him learn colors and numbers. (For a while there, he wanted three red bricks — exactly three, and only red — to take to bed with him each night.)

Our stuff helps us express ourselves. You choose a certain tie to wear to work, you decorate your house a particular way, you take a pottery class and learn how to make a bowl, you read a book, or you use your camera take a picture. We serve other people with our stuff. We use our cars to deliver food to the food pantry. We lace up our running shoes to help raise money for cancer research. We pack up dinner in reusable containers and take it to a neighbor who just had a baby.

Or hospitality: we have more plates than we need for just one family because sometimes we like to have friends over, and we don't think they should have to eat straight off the table. We put clean sheets on the guest-room bed. We buy a grill and a big table for the backyard so that we can throw parties.

Stuff matters, and this is OK.

We practice an incarnational faith. Our faith is lived out in the stories of our lives, which are lived here on earth, in these bodies, which need stuff: chairs to sit on and food to eat and clothes to wear. But living an incarnational faith is tricky, because sometimes all this stuff—this often life-giving stuff—gets in the way, gets twisted around, and instead of becoming life-giving, our stuff becomes life-draining or even downright sinful.

Once upon a time, the Israelites got themselves into some hot water because of their stuff. The story comes to us in Exodus 32, when the Hebrew people are out in the wilderness. This is in that period after they've escaped from Egypt, after the episode with the manna but before they get to the promised land, and Moses has gone up to the mountain to talk with God. He's been gone a long time, and the people start to get a little anxious, a little antsy, and they start to forget all the promises God has made to them. They get Moses' brother Aaron to gather up all their gold—their earrings, their necklaces—and he throws all this in the fire and shapes a golden calf out of it, which the people start to worship.

They start to worship this golden calf instead of the God who brought them out of Egypt. Their stuff—their gold—got in the way and made them forget who they were and where their faith belonged. The gold itself wasn't bad. There's nothing inherently wrong with gold necklaces. But when they take the form of something that interrupts the flow of love between God and God's people, that's trouble.

An example: my smartphone. In a lot of ways, my phone is a gift—it makes my life better. It keeps me connected to friends I haven't seen in a long time. It helps me stay organized. It helps me find my way when I make a wrong turn. I can see photos of my baby nephew who lives seven hundred miles away and won't be a baby much longer.

In a lot of other ways, though, it's not so much a gift. It means I'm connected to my e-mail. All. The. Time. I'm always checking to see if someone is doing something cooler than what I'm doing. Sometimes I pay more attention to my phone than I do to my kids.

It's not the phone's fault.

Sometimes our stuff is a blessing.

Sometimes it's a curse.

Which reminds me of another time when the Israelites were out in the wilderness, this time just on the verge of the promised land, and Moses, who knows he won't live to see them enter their new home, gives a sort of farewell speech. He says to them: "I call heaven and earth as my witnesses against you right now: I have set life and death, blessing and curse before you. Now choose life—so that you and your descendants will live" (Deut. 30:19 CEB).

Life and death, blessing and curse.

Sometimes our stuff—our food, our clothes, our houses, our phones—is blessing; sometimes it's curse. Sometimes it's life; sometimes it's death.

So: choose life, and not just for ourselves, but for everybody.

After my most recent Costco excursion, I unloaded the back of the car and carried the boxes into the kitchen, feeling the sense of accomplishment I always do when I finish the weekly shopping. (*Look, I did something! I acquired these goods needed for the survival of my family!* It's as if I've trekked out to the forest and caught dinner with my own two hands.)

As I unpack, I finally put my finger on one of the feelings I'd had as I roamed the overstuffed aisles. It's like I've been disloyal. Like I'm cheating. Can I value small, local, community, and still buy my toilet paper in bulk? Can I shop at Costco on Friday afternoon and still show my face at the farmers' market Saturday morning?

I've heard that Costco treats its employees well, that it's a decent place to work. They made a point of not opening on Thanksgiving Day and hold reasonable hours the rest of the year. They may encourage you to buy a jug of orange juice big enough to feed an army, but at least they don't try to get you to do it at ten o'clock at night.

And, for the most part, the prices are good. If I'm going to buy grapes shipped across the country to put in the kids' lunch boxes (and, let's face it, I am), shouldn't I get the best deal I can? Make the most of the grocery budget?

What I'm wondering is this: We're going to have stuff. Is there a reasonable, responsible, sustainable, faithful way to acquire it? How do we make sure our stuff is a blessing and not a curse, to ourselves, our neighbors, and the earth?

Because even when our stuff is life-giving to us, it may be just the opposite to the people who made it possible for us to have it. Like the migrant farmworkers who earn way less than minimum wage for their work that brings inexpensive produce to my grocery store and helps me keep my family healthy. Or the workers in foreign factories who work in unsafe, even life-threatening conditions to make the clothes that keep my kids warm in the winter. Or the people in countries wracked by war and human-rights atrocities who bring us the minerals that make our cell phones work and keep us connected to people we love.

Blessing or curse?

Writer Ellen Painter Dollar pondered these questions, too, as she and her family went through a major remodeling of their home. They made some intentional, sustainable choices: bought furniture from a local manufacturer,

used environmentally friendly materials, gave away usable appliances instead of throwing them away.

"But," she writes, "we still produced a dumpster full of waste. I bought several things, such as dishtowels and throw pillows, at chain stores that could very well be procuring goods from foreign factories with questionable labor practices. I could have avoided these questionable purchases by making my own throw pillows or, more significantly, living indefinitely with the outdated but essentially functional kitchen we already had."[1]

This "mix of responsible and ethically questionable" decisions, Dollar notes, is, in some ways, simply a symptom of living in an imperfect and broken world, and if we are to live faithfully and well, we are called to do what we can, acknowledge the ways we fall short, and keep trying all the same.[2]

Laura Hartman, in her book *The Christian Consumer*, says something similar as she lays out a helpful approach to responsible consumption. First—perhaps at once most obvious and most difficult—our challenge is to avoid sin: the sins of greed, gluttony, exploitation, ecological destruction. Second, a faithful Christian will consume in ways that embrace creation, by celebrating the gifts of creation and caring for the earth. Third, we make choices that help us love our neighbor; we build relationships and figure out how our neighbors—near and far—are affected by our choices. Finally, we envision the future, looking always forward to the time when God will heal our broken world.[3]

It will never be clear-cut; we'll never have easy answers. But perhaps if we keep all that in mind, we'll move a little closer toward choosing life, for ourselves and for the world.

∞∞

The good news is that as more people are paying attention to the impact of our purchases, there are more opportunities for making responsible choices. A few years ago, you could

find coffee and tea that was Fair Trade Certified, and occasionally some fancy chocolate, but that was about it. Now, though, there are a whole variety of fair-trade products, from bananas and olive oil to jewelry, shoes, and clothes.

Sometimes people get free trade and fair trade mixed up, but they are totally different things, and the difference is important. Advocates of free trade think that goods and services should be priced at whatever the market will bear, regardless of any other considerations. The area of North Carolina where I live, which was long known for its textile manufacturing, was hit hard when free-trade policies made it cheaper for factories to move to other countries. All over town, now, you'll find abandoned textile mills and people whose lives were changed by the loss of jobs.

On the other hand, a product that is fairly traded is given a price point that takes into account the wages and working conditions of the people who grew or created it. Sometimes that means your cup of coffee is a little more expensive, but it also means that the coffee growers get to feed their families.

Taylor McCleneghan works for Mata Traders, a fair-trade clothing company that works with local artisan groups in India and Nepal. The clothes, which are sold in the United States, are handmade by women's cooperatives that practice fair-trade principles like paying a living wage, providing child care, and maintaining safe working conditions. Mata Traders develops long-term relationships with the local producers, working with them to make quality products that benefit everybody involved.

McCleneghan, who has been with Mata Traders for a while now, said that it's been heartening to see some bigger clothing companies start to care more about fair trade and other considerations beyond the bottom line. She says it will take all of us making small steps in the right direction for real change to happen. That means looking up the corporate responsibility statements of our favorite stores and making a point of choosing fair trade whenever possible.

It's complicated, she told me, but it's just not OK to be complacent about how things are.

I ordered a couple of Mata dresses last summer — they're darn cute, if I do say so myself — but fair trade isn't the answer for all our purchasing, at least not yet. Fun summer dresses are great, but when I need a suit for one of those days when I have to look particularly grown-up and professional, I'm usually still stuck with the more traditional stores. In those cases, I can do some research and patronize a company that has at least shown some indication that they care about people and the planet as well as profits. And more and more, I've gotten lucky and found some good-quality used clothes at a couple of my favorite local thrift shops.

Speaking of thrift stores, what about the stuff we have no use for anymore? A couple of times a year, Rob and I haul a van full of giveaway stuff to our friendly Goodwill store. Since I've become a more regular thrift-store shopper, I've gotten a little more discriminating about what we give away and what we just throw in the trash. If I don't want that broken-beyond-repair lamp or that white sweater with a big brown stain on the front, it's likely that nobody else does, either. It's made me more aware of taking better care of our stuff, with the hopes that somebody else will be able to use it when we pass it along. It's also worth noting, though, that Americans donate way more clothing to thrift stores than the stores can deal with — it's not just that we need to take better care of our stuff; we also need a lot less stuff to begin with.

CO CD

I wish there were some simple rules to all this. Some kind of definitive explanation of what "ethically sourced" actually means, some sort of checklist to let us know if a product is OK to buy. Does it count if the materials were acquired here but assembled overseas? Made in a sweatshop but sold at a local boutique? What if it's fair-trade coffee sold at a big-box store? Like everything else, it's complicated.

Let me tell you another story about sleds.

While I have now lived below the Mason-Dixon Line for more than a decade, I'm a midwestern girl at heart. I can't say I don't love the long seasons of fall and spring, or the mild winters, of North Carolina, but I do still feel a pang of jealousy when I see pictures of my northern friends playing in the snow. That artificial ice-slide at the downtown rink each winter is a poor substitute for the real thing.

The hill I went sledding on growing up in Indiana—a state not known for its hilly terrain—was called Chicken Hill, by the way, presumably because you had to be a really big chicken not to try it, seeing as it was little more than a gentle slope between the cemetery and the golf course.

My poor southern-born children have had few opportunities to play in the snow, much less go sledding, despite the fact that there is a perfect sledding hill behind Harper's elementary school, within walking distance from our house. It's not even all that easy to find a sled around here. We borrowed one from a friend a couple years ago, just for an afternoon, and we have my dad's fifty-year-old wooden Radio Flyer, which is awesome but which doesn't work so well in North Carolina's rare and icy snow.

So, when I was out Christmas shopping one day in early December and I happened to see a stack of plastic saucer sleds in a bin outside a big-box store, I decided my kids needed to have them.

The sleds I saw clearly were included in this store's inventory under the "beyond" category, having nothing to do with beds or baths. I could tell they were cheap without even lifting one. But even cheap plastic sleds last a while, especially when you use them only once or twice a season. So if I bought these cheap sleds, we would be stuck with them forever.

It would have been the perfect Santa gift—straight from the snowy North Pole to our temperate clime, so big and colorful under the tree Christmas morning—but I couldn't bring myself to buy them. In my mind, these cheap plastic sleds fell squarely in the category of the sort of "crap" I really don't want in our house.

So I didn't buy them. Instead, I congratulated myself on deciding on the perfect Santa gift and resolved to buy some sleds at the locally owned toy store where I buy birthday presents for my kids' friends.

This made sense in my mind, as if it fit somehow in my Rules for Buying Stuff. I can't exactly tell you what the rules are, but the list goes something like this:

Buy it used if at all possible.
Buy it local and handmade, usually, unless it's really expensive.
Buy it fair-trade if it's available.
If you're going to buy Cheap Plastic Crap, buy it from a locally owned store. (And our local toy store has its share of Cheap Plastic Crap, but it also has slightly better quality plastic crap.)
Sometimes, buy Cheap Plastic Crap from a big-box store.
But not very often.

Like I said, it's a little slippery.

Anyway, I was OK with buying the sleds from the toy store. Except, they didn't have any when I stopped by that afternoon, about three weeks before Christmas.

And they didn't have any that weekend when I went in to buy a birthday present.

Or when I called the next week.

"We might get some in soon," the clerk kept saying.

But they didn't have any on the evening of December 22, either, when I slipped out of the house to do that last-minute shopping that I always swear I'm not going to do but always have to anyway. The store was buzzing with people grabbing up toys, and the worker I snagged with his hands full of boxes looked at me with a bit of pity when I asked if they might get any more sleds in. "Not before Christmas."

So.

By now, in my mind, this quest for these sleds had all the makings of a Hallmark holiday special: the only thing these children want for Christmas is a sled (actually, they hadn't even thought of sleds), and if this frantic mother can't find some, there will be nothing (except the seven million boxes that had been delivered to our house from friends and family in the past three weeks) under the tree on Christmas morning!

Back I went to the big-box store. The sleds were still there. I bought two.

And then second-guessed myself all the way home.

I explained the dilemma to Rob, who had been following, with his usual patient tolerance, the drama of the sleds for the past few weeks. "I just didn't want to give them cheap plastic crap," I whined to him as he put the dishes away.

"So, let's take them back," he said. "There is no shortage of gifts around here. Something else can be the Santa gift. We'll get sleds at the toy store when they do come in, and we can keep them in the shed until it snows, and it'll be a special surprise then."

And he, the hero of this Christmas story, braved the shopping center parking lot on Christmas Eve to return the Cheap Plastic Crap to the big-box store.

My point is this: In the hierarchy of flexible, slippery rules, sometimes we have to stop somewhere. It's OK to do without. It's not enough to whine that I couldn't find locally sourced sleds and then just go ahead and buy the others. Doing without has to be OK sometimes. That's what trusting in enough is all about. That, I think, is choosing life. Blessing, not curse.

It is not inevitable that we shop at Costco. We choose to do so. I don't have to buy grapes for the kids' lunches. We could do without. I have to be honest about this, that I have so many choices, that I don't get to abdicate responsibility.

I like what Ellen Painter Dollar says about doing what we can, confessing when we fall short, and doing our best anyway. And I like what Hartman has to say about avoiding sin, embracing creation, loving neighbor, and looking toward the future. So here's what I think that looks like, down and dirty, in the midst of our everyday lives. Here's what it means to choose life when it comes to our stuff.

First, we don't take our stuff for granted—we remember that it all comes from God, that it's all a gift from God. Sometimes it's easy to remember that when we look at grand sunsets or beautiful mountains, but what if we also remembered, every morning when we're getting dressed, that even our shoes are a gift from God?

We don't let our stuff control us. Sure, we use our smartphones to stay connected, but maybe we don't let our phones take over. We turn off the e-mail at night or once a week. We leave it at home when we go to the playground. We think of the rich, young man who had so many possessions that he couldn't imagine letting them go, and we remind ourselves that we're in charge, not our stuff. We pay attention to enough.

We use our stuff to nurture delight. Our stuff helps us enjoy and celebrate the gift of life. We share meals with friends, and we bring out the best dishes. We dress up for special occasions. We give gifts to people we love.

We find ways to use our stuff to make life better for other people. We take good care of what we have so that we can share it, and we use what we have to help somebody out.

We make sure our stuff doesn't interrupt the flow of love between us and God or us and other people. That means paying attention to where and how our stuff was made and where we buy it; it means making sure our stuff—even our life-giving stuff—isn't life-draining or life-threatening for somebody else.

That manna in the wilderness was life-giving stuff. It sustained the people, not forever, but for the day ahead. It was enough, and it was a gift from God. It was life, not death. It was blessing, not curse.

Living with God's abundance doesn't mean overflowing shopping carts. It is trusting in enough and choosing life.

Then you and your descendants will live.

CHAPTER 8

―――――― ⟡ ――――――

SABBATH

In the western highlands of Scotland, not far from Loch Lomond, midway between Glasgow and the Isle of Skye, the A83 highway winds its way up a steep and windy route and peaks at an overpass that has become known as Rest and Be Thankful.

Restandbethankful, as if it is all one word. That was the inscription on a monument placed there by the soldiers who built the road back in 1753, but the path had been well worn before that by generations of travelers who needed to cross from one side of the ridge to the other.

The name of the place is part command and part per-mission: After that long, hard climb, it is good—maybe even necessary—to stop and rest your weary legs, or let your horses have a drink of water, or—nowadays—let the car engine cool off. Rest, and be thankful that you made it.

If we are going to find a new way to live, if we are going to live a life that is oriented toward care for earth and neighbor, we're going to be swimming upstream a little bit. We're going to be making some countercultural choices about the stuff we buy and the money we spend, the way we live our lives, so we're going to need some help. We're going to need some practices that will sustain us for the long haul. Lament and confession are a couple of those practices; nurturing hope and delight are others. (More on those soon.) Sometimes it's going to feel like we're climbing up a mountain, and we'll need a spot to take a breather, to rest and be thankful. Practicing Sabbath just might be the rest stop we need.

∞

In the beginning, God created.
God saw that it was good.
On the seventh day, God rested.

This is how the world was made, a rhythm of work and rest, Sabbath woven right into the very fabric of creation.

∞

I have to confess that I don't always love dinnertime these days. I like to cook, and I don't mind the grocery shopping and the meal planning, but the process of getting everybody in the family (and there are only four of us!) to the table at the same time, with hands washed and a minimal amount of bickering about who is sitting where, is exhausting. I sometimes find myself yearning for the days before kids when dinner didn't have to be such a production and I could eat a bowl of cereal on the couch if I wanted to.

But then, usually, we all finally sit down and somebody says grace. It's not always peaceful and serene; sometimes our dinner blessings involve loud singing and banging on the table, and it's not unusual for somebody to fall out of his or her chair. But we stop for a minute, the four of us, and we name our gratefulness. It is, I'm discovering, a small moment of Sabbath rest.

Breathe in, breathe out. Rest, and be thankful.

A deep breath before dinner is a far cry from the full day of rest decreed by God, however. The Sabbath shows up first there in Genesis, when the world is created, but by the time the Israelites find themselves freed from slavery and wandering in the wilderness, it becomes a command. It's the fourth of the Ten Commandments, and its placement near the center of the list is no coincidence.

The first three commandments are about God and our relationship with the Divine—that God should be our only god, that all our worship and honor should go to the one true God who brought us out of Egypt. The last six commandments are about our relationship with other people. Be good to your family. Don't kill each other. Don't cheat or steal or lie or be jealous of other people's stuff. And right in the center there, between the commandments about living with God and the commands about living with other people, is that bit about keeping the Sabbath.

I keep coming back to Walter Brueggemann, who talks about the Sabbath as a connector, a bridge of sorts, between our relationship with God and our relationship with people. To understand what he says, though, we have to go all the way back to the Hebrew people when they were still in Egypt. They were slaves, of course, working for Pharaoh, who, Brueggemann says, was running one of the biggest production systems in history. Pharaoh was interested in building more and bigger things, and he needed this slave labor to do it as cheaply as possible. So he worked these slaves hard and pushed them to work faster and produce more, and this is why he was so adamant that they not leave—if he lost this free labor, he wouldn't be able to get nearly as much done.

They lived in this culture of doing more, working more, getting more. Sound familiar?

But then God leads them out of Egypt, across the Red Sea and into the wilderness, where they take on this new life, this new identity—they are no longer slaves but the free people of God. Figuring out what that means is tricky, so God gives them some guidelines, some commandments, about how to live with God and how to live with people, and there in the middle is Sabbath.

Back in Egypt, they weren't free to take a break. They couldn't stop working. They lived in a system of scarcity, a system of anxiety, where Pharaoh demanded more and more. There was no Sabbath keeping to be had. But now: They are free. Free to trust in God's abundance. Free to observe the Sabbath, to rest—as God did when the world began. They—we—are the people of God, not Pharaoh, and that's the life God calls us to. "Sabbath," Brueggemann says, "becomes a decisive, concrete, visible way of opting for and aligning with the God of rest."[1]

But what does Sabbath keeping look like for twenty-first-century Americans?[2] Our bodies need physical rest— or if we've been sitting in office chairs all week, we need to move. We need to play and to read something just for fun. We need to go outside and breathe real air and notice that we are one small part of this incredible created world.

Our eyes and minds need a break from the screens we stare at most of the day. This is a growing edge for me: As much as I appreciate the Internet's ability to keep me connected to friends and family and to provide me with any piece of information I could possibly wish for, I have to confess that browsing online rarely leaves me feeling rested, nor does it foster gratitude in me very often. Envy, yes, when I see pictures of friends at a get-together I'm too far away to attend. Greed, yes, when I see a cute pair of boots on sale. Self-loathing, yes, when other people's lives look more interesting/simple/tidy/faithful/productive/generous than mine. A regular break from all that is important, a screen Sabbath that grounds me back in my 3-D life and reminds me that I have what I need right here.

The same goes for taking a time-out from buying stuff or spending money at all. I know people who have practiced a "buy nothing new" month, and I like the idea of trying to make it at least one day a week without using the car.

Sabbath gives us a chance to disengage from the system, even briefly, so that we remember we are not enslaved to it.

But the significant thing about Sabbath keeping is that it's not just for our own benefit, as luxurious as a whole day of rest sounds to this busy mama. The Sabbath is not just for us; it's for the world.

> Remember the sabbath day, and keep it holy. Six days you shall labor and do all your work. But the seventh day is a sabbath to the LORD your God; you shall not do any work — you, your son or your daughter, your male or female slave, your livestock, or the alien resident in your towns.
>
> — Exod. 20:8–10

Look at who should keep Sabbath: you. But also: your sons and daughters, your servants, your livestock, and anybody else who happens to live nearby.

In other words, Sabbath is not just for you, but for everybody around you. The whole community. Brueggemann says that this is a call for an entire system of rest and abundance — which is way different from the system of anxiety and production the Hebrew people had just left behind.

If we took that seriously, would we act any different in our Sabbath time? Would we maybe not do things that require other people to work? Eating dinner out might give you a break from the dishes, but somebody's got to do them. Maybe we ought to start to think about what Sabbath would look like if it was for all of God's people, and not just us.

Because increasingly, people aren't free to practice the Sabbath. If you have to work two or three jobs to make ends meet for your family, then time to stop and rest is probably hard to come by. And as more and more companies are turning to contract workers instead of full-time employees, more and more people don't have the benefit of paid time off. Part of Sabbath keeping and living well, then, is advocating for a living wage so that all God's people can be free to rest.

Sabbath rest is not just a practice of self-care, but also care for creation and care for neighbor. That's why its placement in the center of the Ten Commandments is so important: it's right at the heart of loving God and loving neighbor.

☙❦❧

There's nothing much there at the top of that pass in the highlands of Scotland, at Rest and Be Thankful. There's a bench, a sign marking the spot, a picnic table. The view is gorgeous, to be sure. But nobody goes to Rest and Be Thankful just for the sake of going there. It's a place you pass through on the way to something else.

Sabbath keeping isn't a destination. It's a stopping point along the way.

You climb the mountain, admire the view, catch your breath a minute, and then head on out to wherever you're heading, on to whatever new road awaits.

We stop to catch our breath, and then we go on our way. But we return often, because it is the source of our strength and our hope, and our reminder that we are free, that we are connected to one another, and that none of us do this alone.

We need the sort of Sabbath rest that grounds us in our community, our home, and our faith story. Sabbath keeping reminds us that we are not essential for the spinning of the earth and makes us aware of the other people who make our lives possible. Sabbath keeping is no simple indulgence; it is a practice vital to our humanity and to our life together.

Breathe in, breathe out. Rest, and be thankful.

CHAPTER 9

──────────── ⟨⟩ ────────────

STRANGER TO
NEIGHBOR

Go and Do Likewise

The day after Ash Wednesday, on the way to Nicaragua, I changed planes in Miami. The flight to Managua was huge and crowded, with at least three groups on board that were clearly on their way to mission trips. My seat, by a window near the back of the plane, was smack in the middle of one of the groups, and the row behind me was full of college-age girls swapping corny Christian jokes. There were only three seats in a row, but somehow it felt like there were more of them back there. There was a lot of giggling. (I am old. And a party pooper, apparently.) By the end of the flight, they had corralled a young woman in my row into translating for them, and they all were loudly trying to figure out what some word means. I was glad to have my headphones.

When we got off the plane, the groups were congregating near customs, their leaders trying to check everybody in, counting noses, getting ready for the next step in the process. I gratefully slipped by them and made it through to baggage claim by myself.

Nicaragua is a poor country, the second poorest in the hemisphere, next to Haiti. The country's poverty combined with its proximity to the United States—the flight from Miami takes only a few hours, and the capital city, Managua, is in the same time zone as Chicago—make it a popular destination for mission trips from the States.

Before I left, my guidebook warned me, "Nicaragua has Central America's lowest crime rate . . . but in a country where many workers make the equivalent of $2 a day, you'll represent enormous wealth." No doubt about it: between my laptop, my camera, and my cell phone, I had a couple thousand dollars in electronic equipment alone.

Later in the trip, I realized I'd been seeing a number of big yellow school buses in the midst of the city traffic. When I asked one of my hosts about it, he told me they are decommissioned school buses from the United States, donated or sold and driven to Central America and used for municipal or private transportation.

"So, when the buses are deemed too old or too unsafe for American kids, they get used here?"

"Yep," he said. And judging from the look of the bus we were passing, they've gotten lots of years of use.[1]

The relationship between the United States and its poorer global neighbors is a complex one, so much so that even the terminology gets complicated. Sometimes we call it the first world and the third world (those are throwback terms from the Cold War, by the way: the first world was the United States and its buddies; the second world was all the Communist countries, with whom U.S. relationships were ideologically—and sometimes physically—hostile; and the third world was everybody else), sometimes we refer to developed and developing countries, sometimes it's the global north and the global south (given that a majority of the world's wealth and resources reside in the Northern Hemisphere). In almost every case—the United States being an odd exception—those divisions also indicate the difference between former colonies and the countries who colonized them. Almost inevitably, we default to the terms "us" and "them."

This us/them language is understandable when we consider how we talk about missions and service in the church—"we" who have a lot need to help "them" who do not—but it's also problematic. Sometimes that binary division carries the implicit message that we are not just different from "them" but also superior. We talk about serving "the hungry," "the poor," "the needy" in a way that reduces "the poor" to a faceless, nameless, generic "other." We love to quote that passage from Matthew 25, in which Jesus says that anytime we care for the "least of these," we care for him. But we seem to forget that Jesus didn't often speak in such generic terms. Usually, the Gospels tell us about encounters with individual people, each facing individual problems, whom Jesus heals, tends to, welcomes, and feeds. The woman at the well, the man with an unclean spirit, Jairus's daughter, Mary and Martha and Lazarus, Simon's mother-in-law, the hemorrhaging woman, the blind man, all people who stop being "them" when Jesus walks alongside them.

Take the Good Samaritan story (Luke 10:25–37)—it's the classic do-gooder story of the Bible, acted out in nearly every church camp or vacation Bible school program I've ever been a part of. Jesus tells the story to a lawyer who—like the rich young man—wants to know what it takes to get this life that Jesus has been preaching about. He knows the greatest commandment: to love God with heart, soul, strength, and mind, and to love your neighbor as yourself. But he's stumped, he tells Jesus, about who this neighbor is.

Instead of answering the question, Jesus, in characteristic style, tells a story about a man who'd been attacked by robbers. The shocking part of this story is not that a Levite and a priest don't stop to help the man who has been beaten up and left for dead. The shocking part is that a Samaritan does. To the Jews of Jesus' time, Samaritans were the ultimate "them." The Samaritan's care for the beaten-up man—each of them individuals, with a story, not generic groups of people—answers the question of who the neighbor is. Jesus tells the lawyer, then, to "go and do likewise."

In my own congregation—which is full of generous, good-hearted people—we spend a whole lot of time and effort donating money and food to help hungry people we'll probably never meet. I have no doubt that this is important, worthwhile work that helps meet needs in our community. But it does little to break down the wall between the "us" who have food to spare and the "them" who do not.

Thinking in us/them terms can become a problem in a couple of ways. That distance between us and them can keep "us" from recognizing what the real issues are. We might feel good about donating food so that a school kid has something to eat at home on the weekends, but if we never get to know that kid—if he's always a "them"—then we might not understand that the reason he doesn't have food at home is that his mother can't work because she can't afford child care for his baby sister, and his dad is working a job that doesn't have any benefits, so sometimes they have to choose between food and medication. Keeping the other at arm's length means that we don't have to look at the big picture and consider what might need to change.

When the "them" lives in a different part of the world, it's even easier to ignore the individuality of people's lives and to group everybody together in an unnamed "other." For a long time, the pattern of relationship between North American Christians and the rest of the world has been something like this: Christians, inspired by the knowledge that we're financially better off than a lot of the world and by Jesus' commands to "be witnesses to the ends of the earth," send people and money to poorer countries to help. Depending on one's theology and tradition, sometimes that means sending missionaries to convert the "natives" to Christianity. Sometimes it means sending a group to build houses or dig wells in an attempt to improve the lives of the people there. It usually involves a lot of fund-raising and planning on the part of tired youth ministers who have to track down permission forms from teenagers, and inevitably, after the trip, there's some kind of church dinner and a slide show. Almost always, someone says, "I went there to help, but I got so much more out of it than I gave."

I've always felt a bit conflicted when I hear stories about international mission trips like this, but it's only recently that I've been able to articulate why. When we use phrases like "such a good experience" and "got so much more than we gave," it sounds an awful lot like maybe we're in it for ourselves. Too often, such trips serve to reinforce stereotypes, increase dependency on foreign assistance, and serve as a sort of "poverty tourism" for the travelers. Yes, as people who are committed to following the way of Jesus, we ought to be concerned with feeding the hungry, clothing the naked, and taking care of the poor. But we ought to do it in a way that is actually helpful to the hungry, naked, and poor, and not just in a way that makes us full, clothed, rich people feel better.[2]

So, what are we supposed to do? What would actually be helpful? How are we supposed to love our neighbors? How should we care for the least of these? How do we go and do likewise?

∞∞∞

Rebecca Todd Peters has written a lot about the ethics of globalization, exploring the faithful ways we live in a world in which we are more deeply connected to our global neighbors than ever before. In her book *Solidarity Ethics*, she offers a helpful commentary on the way we respond to needs in the world by describing three "categories of moral intuition."

Our initial response to need, she says, is *sympathy*. "Primarily, people who respond from a moral intuition of sympathy are motivated either by feelings of pity and sorrow for the misfortunes of others, or by the guilt they feel when they judge that their lives are 'better' than the lives of those they reach out to help."[3] While good and right, stopping at this response ignores questions of systemic dysfunction — why is there such inequality in the first place? — and, perhaps more dangerously, begins to imply that privileged people are somehow morally superior and have been therefore more "blessed" than their poorer neighbors.

When I talked with Peters in person about all this, she said to me, "We really need to develop a new theology of blessing." It's such a tricky word; of course we want to call our gifts blessings and ascribe them to a generous God. But then what about those who are not similarly "blessed"? Are they not also loved and cared for by this same God? Is God not as generous with them?

A second category of response, slightly more nuanced than simple sympathy, is *responsibility*. We who have a lot begin to recognize our own privilege and our own complicity in the problems in the world. This is a step in the right direction, but it can lead to a paternalistic attitude toward helping: "We" are responsible and therefore must fix "their" problems. Peters writes: "God did not endorse an ethic of paternalism by telling people to love their neighbors as they love their children; rather, the commandment to 'love your neighbor as yourself' is a commandment of equality, which forms the foundation of an ethic of solidarity."[4]

Ideally what we ought to be working toward, Peters suggests, is a third response, that of *mutuality*, or solidarity, in which "people act to help others out of an understanding that the well-being of all creation is interdependent."[5] That is, we need to be in relationship with one another.

I think of Becca and Paul, the friends I visited who had built the straw house and had their water carried up the hill by oxen. They've made their lives among the people of Nicaragua. They live and work and serve alongside their neighbors, in relationship with them in a way they never could be if they came to visit only for a week.

Which is not to say that we should all move to a poorer country and take up residence. We're not all called to that. Nor does it mean that we should abandon mission trips completely. Sometimes, it's a short-term mission trip that inspires someone to move from sympathy (for the poor people we are coming to help) to responsibility (asking what bigger systems are at play that are causing this inequality) to mutuality (real and lasting relationships with our neighbors). What we need are opportunities that push us to interact with our neighbors in ways that transform our understanding of the world and move us to action and deepened relationship.

⚭

My first night in Nicaragua was hot. Actually, every night in Nicaragua was hot. The days, too. Back home, a late winter ice storm had hit central North Carolina the day I left, knocking down trees and power lines and canceling school for several days. Fanning myself in Laura Jean's un-air-conditioned living room, it was sort of surreal to watch Facebook posts from friends whose cars were covered with ice and who had been without electricity for days.

I shared a room with Maya, Tim and Laura Jean's two-year-old, who very helpfully unpacked my entire suitcase at least three times while I was there. Quinn—their older daughter, the one born the same time as Harper—had vacated her space and moved in with her parents so that I could have a bed. I woke up, sweating, that first night, to find that Maya had escaped from her crib and was staring at me, wondering about this stranger who had taken over her sister's bed. The next day, in the slightly cooler shade of the backyard, I watched Maya and Quinn play with buckets of water, getting muddy and wet and laughing. I listened to Quinn chatter away in fluent Spanish to her Nicaraguan friends and felt a pang of regret that I hadn't kept up what little Spanish I learned in high school.

I'm not sure I did one helpful thing while I was there. Surely I offered to help with the dishes one night, but I suspect that lugging my camera around and making my friends translate every interaction did very little good for anybody but me. This wasn't intended to be a mission trip; there was no construction work planned — I'm lousy with a hammer, anyway — but there was a fair amount of late-night conversation about theology and the ethics of responsible missions. (This is what old friends from seminary do for fun. Jealous, aren't you?)

During their time in Nicaragua, Tim and Laura Jean had hosted a number of mission-trip groups from the United States, some better at navigating the terrain than others. They understood the importance of these trips as one piece in the puzzle of the continuing long-term relationships that made their work possible.

It was Tim who first pointed me to a powerful article called "Rethinking Service," written by Samuel Wells, former dean of the chapel at Duke University. In it, Wells argues that we have generally understood the primary problem of the human condition to be mortality. If that's the case, then a service ethic of *for* makes sense: we want to do as much *for* our neighbors to ease their pain and suffering as we can. But perhaps, he suggests — as Peters does when she articulates an ethic of solidarity — the primary human problem is instead *isolation*, and what our neighbors need most is for us to be *with* them so that none of us are alone. Wells writes:

"For" is a fine word, but it does not dismantle resentment, it does not overcome misunderstanding, it does not deal with alienation, it does not overcome isolation.

Most of all, "for" is not the way God relates to us. God does not simply set the world straight for us. God does not simply shower us with good things. God does not mount up blessings upon us and then get miserable and stroppy when we open them all up and fail to be sufficiently excited or surprised or grateful. "For" is not the heart of God. . . .

But God shows us something else. God speaks a rather different word. In Matthew's gospel, the angel says to Joseph, "'Behold, the virgin shall conceive and bear a son, and they shall name him Emmanuel,' which means, 'God is with us.'" And then in John's gospel, we get the summary statement of what the Christian faith means: "The Word became flesh and lived with us." It is an unprepossessing little word, but this is the word that lies at the heart of Christmas and at the heart of the Christian faith. The word is "with."[6]

So, if we are going to live out this good news, if we are to be Christ's witnesses to the ends of the earth, we had better not stop at *for* but move toward *with*.

Global Ministries, the missions ministry of the Christian Church (Disciples of Christ), calls this the work of "accompaniment" (as do others who think about doing mission work responsibly and faithfully). To accompany is to walk alongside. Missionaries who practice a ministry of accompaniment work with local organizations, come only when invited, and listen to what the local folks need. In other words, it's about building a long-term relationship. It's working *with*. This is how Tim and Laura Jean are doing mission work in Nicaragua. They're part of an established church, working with a local church, doing what needs to be done in the most helpful way possible, with the people there. Laura Jean works with her students, teaching theology and training pastors; Tim works with community groups to install those sci-fi biodigesters.

In a piece she wrote a while back, Laura Jean says, "The mainline groups [like Global Ministries] have come to trust their local partners, realizing that in matters practical as well as spiritual, we have a great deal to learn from sisters and brothers around the world."[7]

My dad is a retired pastor, and he and my mom have done a fair bit of traveling to visit Global Ministries mission projects, which was probably my first introduction to the fact that there are different ways of interacting with our global neighbors. When I was in fifth grade, they left my sister and me with our grandparents and traveled to Africa for three weeks. (Those were the days before the Internet, and I don't think we had any contact with them the whole time they were gone. When Rob and I went to Spain last summer, we e-mailed the kids at least once a day, and we were gone for six days!) When my parents got back from that trip, I remember hearing stories about worshiping with local churches, about meals shared with their hosts. One of the souvenirs they brought home—a small woven rug—still hangs on the wall in their home.

Much more recently, they traveled to India and visited a hospital in the small town of Mungeli, in a remote part of the country that lacks much of the modern infrastructure of the bigger Indian cities. The Disciples have had a presence in the Mungeli community for well over a century, the first missionaries coming to provide Western medical care. Today, the mission supports a growing hospital and nursing school. The hospital is run by Anil and Teresa Henry, both Indian medical doctors serving as Global Missions missionaries. In recent years, the hospital has expanded its technological resources and now provides previously unavailable medical care to the community.

The kind of work that Global Ministries does isn't easy. It's more difficult to build long-term, mutually beneficial relationships than it is to box up our used shoes and ship them overseas. It's flashier and more instantly gratifying to do hands-on service, to fly in for a week and paint a house and come back with pictures to share at the church supper on Wednesday night. (And we *love* instant gratification.) Sending our decommissioned school buses to Central America may provide a means of transportation, but it doesn't do much for developing relationships among neighbors. Sam Wells acknowledges the difficulty, too: "In a lot of ways, 'with' is harder than 'for.' You can do 'for' without a conversation, without a real relationship, without a genuine shaping of your life to accommodate and incorporate the other."[8]

I'm finding that there's sometimes a thin line between *for* and *with*. Like the microfinance Kiva loan Harper and I made a few months ago. She helped me pick out which project to support, and because we started by looking at loans for educational purposes, we ended up making a loan to a young man named Erland who is studying to be a doctor and needed help with books and equipment. That's all well and good, but while it's nice to have a photo of Erland and to know a little of his story, there's no sense in which I am actually in relationship with him at all. It's *for*, not *with*.

On the other hand, the way that organizations like Kiva work *is* substantively different from straight charities that simply give handouts. My Kiva loan gets funneled through a microfinance institution in Nicaragua that works directly *with* Erland. So in a small way, my *for* makes their *with* possible.

My dad, thinking about Dr. Henry and the Mungeli hospital, says that there's an element of community organizing to this kind of accompaniment work. Sometimes the task of the missionary is to mobilize the people who live in a particular community and harness the resources already there. Dr. Henry works *for* and *with* all at the same time.

Most of us are not, probably, going to spend any significant time living in another country. I know that I've never felt called to be a long-term missionary; my life is right here, and I don't see that changing anytime soon. But that doesn't mean I can't be part of *with* work. I can support the church's wider ministry, so that people like Laura Jean and Tim can continue what they're doing. There might be appropriate times and places when giving money, time, and resources make sense. And in whatever congregation or community I'm a part of, we can find ways to make connections with a local church or community in another culture or country or part of the world. We ought to learn from each other, visit when we can, help each other (help can go both ways!), and get to know each other over the long haul.

∞∞

Sandhya Jha, the founder of the Oakland Peace Center in Oakland, California, offers an intriguing alternative to the traditional short-term mission trip. Granted, Oakland's not another country, but it might as well be for as different as it might seem to a white, middle-class church youth group. Participants in the Urban Peace Work Trips work together with Peace Center partners, first learning about the partner organizations and their work in the community and only then going out to do hands-on service. Jha says that the agenda of these trips is not simply to enable privileged mission trippers to come in and help poor people but also to educate them on issues and help them get to know people who are actually doing something to address the really big problems that are no doubt also present in their own communities back home.

The Oakland Peace Center's not alone, of course; there are lots of folks who can help put together a good, healthy mission trip that is more about education and empowerment than it is about quick fixes.

Here in Greensboro, where I live, there's an organization I really admire, FaithAction International House. The mission of FaithAction is to "turn strangers into neighbors," and they do so by providing resources and support for the significant number of immigrants in our community. The people at FaithAction do provide some direct assistance—helping people with past-due rent or an electric bill—but more significantly, they offer opportunities for a diverse population to get to know one another. An intercultural soccer league, for example, brings together players from countries all over the world for friendly competition. A Stranger to Neighbor Dialogue event gathers people for dinner and conversation about where they're from and what their lives are like. A community Thanksgiving celebration showcases entertainment from countries around the world.

The reality of globalization is that the world isn't just out there anymore; the world is here, and we're a part of it. Intentional multicultural efforts like that of FaithAction and others help us get to know our neighbors who are right here, across the street, across town, or around the world.

I've been to a few of the FaithAction events, though not as many as I'd like. Time and inertia, as always, are the roadblocks. I did have a brainstorm the other day, in which I decided that Harper and I should learn Spanish together—her starting from scratch and me dusting off my rusty high school vocabulary—and pair up with some Spanish-speaking folks in town who need to practice their English. Maybe then, Harper and Quinn could talk to each other in Spanish next time we get together. The reality of our lives is that we're going to have to be intentional about connecting across cultural lines, moving from "us and them" to "we," and from "for" to "with."

I wonder if Harper will remember my trip to Nicaragua the way I remember my parents' travels, if it will impact her life in subtle ways. Surely, she will remember the hammock I brought back, and I hope it's around for a while. I also have a new dream of traveling someplace out of the country with our kids sometime before they're totally grown. Not on a mission trip, exactly, but maybe on an educational exchange or to visit a mission station somewhere. It's not just that I want my kids to realize the privileges they have, though I do. More than that, though, I want them to see that our way of living is not the only way, and certainly not the best way. I want them to learn from our neighbors around the world as much as they learn from our neighbors next door.

It occurs to me that what happens in the Good Samaritan story Jesus tells is that the beaten-up man and the Samaritan move from — to borrow FaithAction's phrase — strangers to neighbors. The Samaritan is moved with sympathy and compassion, then claims responsibility in bandaging the man's wounds, and finally, in solidarity with the man, goes with him to the innkeeper and ensures that he will not be alone.

It's possible to do well-meaning work for people who will always remain strangers. The food my congregation grows in our garden and collects on Sunday morning all gets eaten by people we'll probably never meet. That's all fine and good, but we can't stop there. Our compassion should move us to action, and one day, finally, perhaps we'll all work in the garden side by side, no longer strangers but neighbors and friends.

Go, Jesus says, and do likewise.

CHAPTER 10

––––––––––– ⟳⟲ –––––––––––

HOPE

The first Saturday in December was a stay-at-home-and-read-a-book-with-a-cup-of-something-warm-in-your-hands sort of day.[1] It was the kind of damp cold that goes straight to your bones and chills your toes so that they don't get warm for the rest of the day. It was not, by any stretch of the imagination, a good parade-watching day. And yet there we were, lined up outside the library on Church Street, umbrellas in hand, peering down the street and waiting for the sirens to indicate that the holiday parade had started. This is what you do, apparently, when your daughter is walking with her Girl Scout troop in the parade; you get out of your warm slipper-socks and don your raincoat so that you can jump up and down and wave emphatically for the five seconds it takes for her to walk by and grin at you.

Just before the parade started, the rain turned to a drizzle, more annoying than anything else but still unpleasant. Up and down the street were parents and families and the hardiest of holiday revelers, all huddled together for warmth under the gray, oppressive sky.

What are we doing here? I thought to myself. *We should all have agreed to stay home in bed.*

It didn't seem possible that anything cheerful could happen on a day so damp and dark.

⋘⋙

The prologue to the Gospel of John—the closest John comes to any sort of Christmas story—describes Jesus as the light coming into the world: "The light shines in the darkness, and the darkness did not overcome it."

If there was only one sentence to sum up the Christian faith, I think that would be it.

The Gospel of Luke tells the story of Jesus' coming into the world with much less metaphor and much more detail, starting with the arrival of an angel who tells Mary that—despite all evidence to the contrary—she's going to be a mom.

That's when she sings those famous words that became known as the Magnificat.

> "My soul magnifies the Lord,
>   and my spirit rejoices in God my Savior,
>   for he has looked with favor on the lowliness of his servant.
>   Surely, from now on all generations will call me
>   blessed;
>   for the Mighty One has done great things for me,
>   and holy is his name.
>   His mercy is for those who fear him

from generation to generation.
He has shown strength with his arm;
  he has scattered the proud in the thoughts of their
  hearts.
He has brought down the powerful from their thrones,
  and lifted up the lowly;
he has filled the hungry with good things,
  and sent the rich away empty.
He has helped his servant Israel,
  in remembrance of his mercy,
according to the promise he made to our ancestors,
  to Abraham and to his descendants forever.
—Luke 1:46–55

It's an incredible song. Mary isn't saying, *hey, isn't it cool that I'm going to have a baby, let's paint the nursery blue and stock up on diapers.* She's saying, *something is about to happen here that will change the entire world.* This is a song about hope.

Notice the tense she uses to describe what God has done: God "has brought down the powerful from their thrones"; God "has filled the hungry." Even though there are still plenty of powerful people on their thrones, even though there's still a lot of hunger, Mary is proclaiming that the good news has already come.

She names what is at once the toughest and the most promising tenet of our faith: that we live here between the "already" and the "not yet." Christ has already come, and we rejoice—but the world is not yet the place of wholeness and peace that God intends for us. We are in the time between.

I'm starting to realize that I've been thinking about all these human problems—inequality and injustice and hunger—and thinking that we need to find human solutions. If we just tried harder, worked harder, paid more attention, we could fix it. We've somehow created a system in which we know how to produce more than enough food for everyone, but still there are hungry people in the world. We ought to be able to fix that. We dug ourselves into this hole. Can't we find a way out?

That takes some radical changes in how we think about things, though. There's a quote attributed to Albert Einstein that I love: "We cannot solve our problems with the same thinking we used when we created them."

Right? We have to really think differently about how we use our resources, how we live together with the other people we share this planet with, how we live our daily lives. That's hard to do, but it's essential. That's the work we do while we wait. That's how we participate in the coming kingdom of God.

If we start looking for human solutions to all these problems, we're not going to get very far. We can't do this alone.

Did you hear what Mary was singing?

Who shows mercy on everyone from generation to generation?

Who scatters the proud?

Who lifts up the lowly and fills the hungry with good things?

God.

God does this. This is God's work.

There's something remarkable, by the way, about this song Mary sings. It's an awful lot like another song by another mother, years and years before the angel showed up to Mary. This other mother was Hannah, the mother of Samuel, who sings a similar song after she gives birth to a baby boy she thought she'd never have.

Hannah sings:

> The bows of the mighty are broken,
>   but the feeble gird on strength.
> Those who were full have hired themselves out for bread,
>   but those who were hungry are fat with spoil.
>
> —1 Sam. 2:4–5

Hannah gives birth to a baby and the whole world changes.

It's no coincidence that these two mothers are singing the same song. This is the story of how God works in the world: overturning social structures we thought were unassailable, bringing up the lowly and laying low the powerful, feeding the hungry and serving the poor, making the world whole and just again.

Hannah and Mary both know that God is working through them, not just for them, but for the sake of the whole world.

This is how God works. God does this.

I don't say this to let us off the hook. Let me be clear about that: We are not to look at the problems of injustice and inequality and throw up our hands when it gets overwhelming and say, oh well, God will take care of it. It doesn't work that way. Being followers of Jesus means that we're part of the work. Being part of the body of Christ means that we get to be part of the work God is doing here in this world—this hard, dirty, complicated, life-giving work. We've got work to do while we wait.

The faith we affirm is built on the hope of a future reconciliation, a promise that the world will be made whole.

But our faith is also built on the trust that the good news has already happened, is happening now. That's the harder part to see, the harder good news to proclaim, especially when there's no end to injustice.

When there's plenty to go around, but still people don't have enough.

When every choice I make has some negative unintended consequence for someone else.

When it seems that there's no way to live in the world that makes any sense.

When there's nothing but dead ends, that's when we need hope.

Over and over again, God defies what we think is possible and brings new life to a dead-end story.

The flood waters dry up, and Noah looks out from the ark to see a rainbow above dry land.

Abraham and Sarah have a baby long after their bodies are past childbearing age.

The Hebrew people run into the Red Sea with Pharaoh's army close behind, and God makes a way across the water.

In the wilderness, with no food or drink, they're tempted to go back to their lives as slaves, and God rains down manna from heaven.

When they forget what God has done for them, God sends the Ten Commandments and offers a new way of life as the people of God.

When Ruth and Naomi return to Bethlehem barren and alone, God helps them create a family.

Centuries later, when the Hebrew people's homes and their temple have been destroyed by neighboring armies and they've been sent into exile, God promises to always be with them.

When there's no room in the inn, Mary and Joseph find a place to lay their baby.

When Herod threatens the children, God finds a way to keep Jesus alive.

When the Roman soldiers hang him on a cross, God offers up an empty tomb.

New life in a dead-end story.

We are foolish to think that we can fix this broken world ourselves. We are doomed indeed if we think we can find a way ahead on our own.

But nothing is impossible with God, and therein lies our hope.

∞∞

Hope is being able to see that there is light despite all the darkness.

—Desmond Tutu

That rainy day in December when Harper was in the Christmas parade, the sky weighed down on us, heavy and dreary and wet.

But then the parade rounded the corner, and the drums tapped out their cadence and the trumpet fanfare sounded. The baton twirlers twirled, and the parents cheered, and the kids grinned, and the dancers danced as if the sky was blue.

And it occurred to me that putting our hope in God is a little like waiting for a parade in the rain.

The world seems to be swirling ever deeper into chaos, injustice, and terror. And yet, we keep proclaiming that the light is coming, all evidence to the contrary. And then it does, the light comes, sometimes slipping quietly around the corner without much warning, sometimes blasting into our lives with all the fanfare of a big, brass band.

The light shines in the darkness. We wait, and we watch, and when we see it, we cheer as loudly as we can.

CHAPTER 11

———— ⟨⟩⟨⟩ ————

TAKING IT
TO THE STREETS

Voices and Votes

On a sunny Saturday morning in February, we pile into the van and tell the kids we are going on an adventure. All the way to Raleigh, Jonathan asks, "Are we at the 'venture yet?" The bar is low for our family: basically, we decide that anything is an adventure if we head off someplace with snacks packed in the backpack.

This time, we're on our way to the state capital to participate in a rally and march put on by, among others, the state chapter of the NAACP. It's been an interesting time, politically, in North Carolina. When we moved here, Barack Obama had just been elected president and the state had turned blue for the first time. Shortly after, though, the politics started to head red, fast, and now an entirely Republican legislature has made lots of cuts to education and social programs, changed voting laws, and denied Medicaid expansion, among other legislative moves that many of us see as problematic. A growing backlash, fueled in part by the popular Moral Monday events the previous spring, has inspired people from all over the state to converge on the capital and make their opposition known.

Once downtown, we pull into a parking lot and unload the stroller and backpacks. When we unbuckle Jonathan from the car seat, though, we discover an exploding dirty diaper that has contaminated just about every piece of clothing he has on. I thought we were past the diaper-change-in-the-back-of-the-car stage, but apparently not, so we strip him down, clean him up as best we can, and start all over, finally heading out of the parking deck and following the crowds to the rally.

Before we're out of the garage, though, Rob's phone rings. He's just started a new job, and he's on call this weekend, so he heads back to the van to get his laptop and spends the next half hour solving whatever technological crisis has happened this time.

We aren't even there yet, and I'm exhausted. How is this better than staying home?

But then we find some friends, and Rob's call ends and he rejoins us, and the day is pretty, and the energy of the crowd is contagious. There are babies on backs, parents with strollers, old men with banners, college students, church groups, people of every life stage and race, some eighty thousand marchers, a whole throng of people who think maybe the direction our state is headed isn't so good.

During the speeches, I try to explain to Harper why we're here. I tell her we think it's important that teachers and schools have the supplies they need ("Like glue sticks!" she says) and that everybody should be able to vote and have access to good health care. I opt not to explain to her the giant pink uterus held above the crowd by the Planned Parenthood folks behind us.

We stay at the rally until almost lunchtime, when we've exhausted the snacks and we can tell that someone is on the verge of a meltdown, and then we slip down a side street and back to the car and home. We haven't really done anything all morning, just stood and walked and talked, but somehow it feels important all the same.

CO>CO

The thirty-first chapter of Proverbs is best known for its description of a "capable wife" (which kinda makes me want to gag, what with all her perfect children and delicious cooking and beautiful handmade clothes). But what often gets left out of that description are the verses just before it, which only make sense if we know that the whole chapter is a message to King Lemuel from his mother. These are words of wisdom from a mother to her son, probably just before he takes the crown or heads off into battle.

She's giving him advice—decent advice about how to be a good king (that is, until she sets up for her son some pretty unrealistic expectations of a wife, but that's mothers-in-law for you[1]). She says, essentially, don't go messing around, don't drink too much, don't let the spoils of the royal life let you forget what you're there to do. Then, she tells him to:

> Speak out on behalf of the voiceless,
>   and for the rights of all who are vulnerable.
> Speak out in order to judge with righteousness
>   and to defend the needy and the poor.
>   —Prov. 31:8–9 CEB

I love this. I generally think that mothers are sources of great wisdom, anyway, but I particularly love the idea that this king—this powerful king who surely had access to all kinds of other wise advisers—listens to his mother before he heads out into the world.

Moms are so smart.

Speak out on behalf of the voiceless, and for the rights of all who are vulnerable . . . , says the mother to the king.

That queen mother, with those wise words to her son, wasn't just giving him some good advice about playing with the other kids on the playground. She was actually reminding him of the responsibility and role he had as a king. And in that day and age — before democracy, before the Magna Carta and the Declaration of Independence — the role of the king was to uphold the rights of the oppressed. To make sure everybody was taken care of. To act on God's behalf to bring about justice.

She's not just telling him that he should play nicely with others and not let the palace wine go to his head. She's calling him to task and holding him accountable, saying, This is your job: you make sure nobody gets left out or left behind. That's what the government is for.

I tend to think that's still what government is for. And when the government isn't doing it, we need to act like that wise mother and call them — and, ultimately, ourselves — to task.

For us in North Carolina, that means advocating for an expansion of Medicaid so that more people can have access to health care. It means crying foul when the legislature passes discriminatory laws or cuts funding to food stamps and other programs that help people meet some basic needs. It means paying attention when laws are passed that make it harder for people to vote — especially if those people are disproportionately people of color or people who have often had their voices silenced. It means calling on lawmakers to pay our public school teachers better and give the schools the funding they need so that those teachers can actually teach.

If all this is starting to feel a little too political, that's because, well, it's political. "Conserving resources at home and taking on economic and political issues are as inseparable as the yolk and white of a scrambled egg," wrote Doris Janzen Longacre back in 1980. "Once an egg yolk breaks into the white, there's no way to remove every tiny gold fleck. Similarly, once you walk into a supermarket or pull up to a gas pump, you *are* part of the economic and political sphere."[2]

Living a faithful life means participating in the community in which you live, and our communities are governed by politics. In a democracy, the government is us.

∞∞

I'm afraid that those of us who know we have a lot, and are thankful for it, fall into a little trap of feeling grateful and giving out of our gratitude—which is good and right, of course—but sometimes we stop there. Sometimes we stop at gratitude and generosity, and I think we've got to go a step beyond. Sure, we've got to open our hands and share, but we've also got to open our mouths and speak out against the systems that keep our world spinning so incredibly out of alignment with the vision of God's justice that is at the very center of our faith.

That vision of justice is given voice not just by Lemuel's queen mother but also by the prophets, and by Mary's song, and by Jesus himself, who steps into the synagogue in Nazareth, unrolls the scroll of the prophet Isaiah, and reads aloud:

> The Spirit of the Lord is upon me,
>   because he has anointed me
>   to bring good news to the poor.
> He has sent me to proclaim release to the captives
>   and recovery of sight to the blind,
>   to let the oppressed go free,
> to proclaim the year of the Lord's favor.
> —Luke 4:18–19

Jesus is saying that the very reason he has come, the very reason God sent him, is to bring about God's vision of justice, and it's a vision that has everything to do with our political structures, because it has everything to do with how we live together with our neighbors.

Here's an example: You probably give something to your local food bank, and if you're part of a church, your congregation probably does some kind of hands-on service or supports hunger relief efforts in your community. That's all good.

But here's the bigger question: In a country where we have the resources and the technology and the know-how to grow more food than we can possibly eat, how come there are hungry people in the first place? What kind of system have we set up that is so unequal that some people can't meet that very basic need?

God's vision isn't that the rich should feed the hungry. It's that everybody should be able to feed themselves. It's that everybody should have enough. Our gratitude and generosity are essential. But in some ways, charity is just a stopgap measure to hold things together until we work out God's real justice.

So we need to be feeding people. But we also need to be advocating for change.

∞∞

The documentary film *A Place at the Table* tells the powerful story of hunger in modern America.[5] It was hugely helpful to me in understanding why simply stocking food pantries isn't enough, why we need real, systemic change.

I promised that I wouldn't drown you in statistics, but here's one from the film that blew me away: One in two children—that's 50 percent—will be on some kind of food assistance at some point in their lives. One in two!

Also this: Since 1980—which is about when childhood obesity rates began to rise—the price of fruits and vegetables has gone up by 40 percent and the price of processed food has gone down by the same percentage. That means that it's way cheaper to buy a bag of potato chips than it is to buy a bag of fresh apples. Healthy eating is expensive.

There's a reason for this, and it's important to understand. Most of us who don't live on farms don't really pay attention to any of this, but there's a subsidy system that plays a huge role in the way we all eat, whether we know it or not. These agriculture subsidies were set up way back in the 1930s, during the Great Depression, as emergency aid for small family farms in tough economic times. Sometimes you'll hear it referred to as the "farm bill." Those subsidies are still in place, still written into the federal budget, only now they mostly go to major agribusiness, huge farming conglomerates. And here's the rub: those subsidies—that is, taxpayer money—primarily support the producers of corn, soybeans, and wheat, the basic ingredients in highly processed food. Very few subsidies go toward growing fresh fruits and vegetables. That's why processed food is cheap and fresh produce so expensive.

This is a hugely political, and often controversial, issue, and it's just one piece of the puzzle. There's also the issue of the Supplemental Nutrition Assistance Program, called SNAP, the program we used to call "food stamps," which is designed to help struggling families buy food. It really helps some families, but the trouble is that to qualify, a family of three can't make more than $24,000 a year. Anything more than that—which really isn't very much—and they're ineligible for any help. That's when families start turning to churches and community groups to fill in the gaps.

"Charity's a great thing," says Jeff Bridges in *A Place at the Table*. (Yes, The Dude from *The Big Lebowski*. Turns out he's a big advocate for ending childhood hunger.) "But it's not the way to end hunger. We don't fund our Department of Defense through charity. We shouldn't see that our kids are healthy through charity, either."

Public policies around food and hunger matter, and they're worth paying attention to. People aren't going hungry because we don't have enough food. We do have enough food. What we don't have is a system to make sure everybody can afford to eat, and there's no way that churches and small food pantries can keep up with the growing need. We need a much bigger change.

We need to change the subsidy system so that farmers have more incentive to grow healthy food. We need to be more realistic about what it means to live in poverty so that people who need help can actually get it. We need a living wage so that parents can support their families without having to work two or three jobs, and we need equal pay for men and women so that working moms get paid the same as working dads.

What we need is a changed system so that people won't be hungry in the first place.

Because there is enough to go around.

⊙⊙⊙

One of the things I've observed as I watch people who do advocacy work well is that learning about an issue isn't enough. People are always more important than issues, and we're way more likely to care about issues when they affect people we care about. I care about education funding, in part, because I've been to Harper's classroom. I know her teacher and I know how much time she puts in, and I know how many basic classroom things—like printer paper and cleaning products—parents were asked to provide this year because there's just not enough money for supplies.

I care about hunger and homelessness, in part, because of the man named Larry who stopped by the church a few weeks ago in need of a new pair of shoes. He'd been referred to every agency in town, who all sent him to the Goodwill store or Salvation Army—but he pointed down to his feet and said to me, "Those stores don't carry shoes in size 15."

When I talked to Sandhya Jha—she's the one who directs the Oakland Peace Center, where they do those education-based mission trips; she also works to make sure there is affordable housing in one of the most expensive parts of the country—she told me that she cares about housing because she's seen her neighbors, her friends, people she lives with and laughs with and cares about, struggle to meet their rent even though they have solid full-time jobs.

Advocacy work is not just about rallies and protests. When we're paying attention to the big questions behind the problems, even our individual daily choices can take on more meaning. Jha also told me that after she spent time with some people who do agricultural work, she changed some of the choices she makes about her own food. When she learned that the average life expectancy of farmworkers is something like thirty-six years, due to all the chemicals they're exposed to, she realized that buying organic, chemical-free food isn't just something rich people do to make themselves feel healthier. Making the choice for organic food means standing in solidarity with the workers whose lives are affected by that choice. She said, "I wouldn't have made that switch to organics if it hadn't been for that work that brought me into relationship with those farmworkers."

When you care about people, you care about issues. When you care about people, you care about the issues that affect the people you care about—even the ones you'll never meet.

⌒⌒

I want my kids to understand this, that there's more to living faithfully than giving money and stuff away. I want them to know that they're part of a something bigger than themselves and that all of us have a responsibility to be involved.

Later in the spring, a few months after the big Saturday morning rally, I take Harper to Raleigh again.[4] We've left the boys at home this time and joined some other friends for the latest in the series of Moral Monday rallies.

The statehouse in Raleigh is a solid ninety-minute drive from our house, so it makes for a long evening on a school night. Harper is more engaged than I thought she'd be; I'd packed snacks and things for her to do and fully expected to have to bribe her with the promise of ice cream on the way home. But she gets a kick out of holding the signs she and her friend made in the car: "Support our teachers!" one said; the other: "I like my teacher. Pay her more!" Every time someone comes by with a camera, she holds her sign extra high and grins.

As an elementary school kid, her life revolves around school right now; she doesn't understand the complexity of teacher tenure, but she loves her teacher and gets it when we talk about making sure the school has all the support it needs. She doesn't know what Medicaid is, but she knows—especially after her recent bout with an awful case of strep throat—what it means to go to the doctor and get medicine to help her feel better. When the speakers at the rally decry our state's rejection of Medicaid expansion, I whisper to her: "I think everybody should be able to go to the doctor when they're sick; don't you?" She nods.

Whenever a new speaker comes to the microphone, she wants me to pick her up so that she can see over the crowd. I smile to see her singing along with an old civil-rights protest song (and I'm particularly tickled to catch her humming it at home the next day). She claps and chants, and I have to pull her away from the postrally march so that we can head home and get to bed.

One of her favorite refrains these days is, "It's not fair that life's not fair!" Usually, this is in response to my declaration that she may not watch *Frozen* for the third time today. I'm sure, in those whiny moments, that she's thinking of only the grave injustice of being a kid; she's not contemplating public policy. But I'm glad she knows that basic truth: this life isn't fair, and that's not fair. That's why we work for justice. That's why I want to echo the queen mother's words to her son when I say to my own kids: "Speak out on behalf of the voiceless and for the rights of all who are vulnerable."

Despite our recent trips to Raleigh, I've never been a huge fan of political rallies. The nature of a public protest is that there's generally a bad guy, and this time, it's the legislature. I don't want my daughter to come away with the notion that the government, or one particular party, is the enemy or that our lawmakers are bad people. Plus, there's the complicated reality that the legislature was elected by the majority of the people in our state, our neighbors. How do we faithfully engage the people we live and work with? I don't want to exacerbate the already polarizing rhetoric present nearly everywhere. I don't like the "us" vs. "them" divide it sets up.

But when the "them" won't listen and the most vulnerable folks in our state are getting left behind, then I'm grateful for the witness of modern-day prophets like the Rev. William Barber, the North Carolina NAACP president who has spearheaded the Moral Monday movement, who call us to action. Barber writes,

> I believe that deep within our being is a longing for a moral compass. For those of us who are moved by the cries of our sisters and brothers, we know that, like justice, the acts of caring for the vulnerable, embracing the stranger, healing the sick, protecting workers, welcoming and being fair to all members of the human family, and educating all children should never be relegated to the margins of our social consciousness. These are not

just policy issues; these are not issues for some left versus right debate; these are the centerpieces of our deepest traditions of our faiths, of our values, of our sense of morality and righteousness.[5]

As the rally wraps up, Barber leads a group of protesters from the mall toward the Capitol building. Harper and I stand with our friends as the procession passes by, and she gives everybody a thumbs-up. We peel off from the crowd at that point, needing to head back to the car and get home to homework and bedtime. "Why can't we go that way?" she says, pointing to the building where the protesters were heading.

"I don't think they let kids in there," I say, lying a little bit, because *we have to go home to bed* is not going to cut it as a reason to leave the fun, and the truth is they aren't letting anybody in.

She is immediately indignant. "But they're supposed to be making things better for kids!" she cries. "They should let kids in!"

I'm glad for her to know that she has a voice and that, eventually, she'll have a vote. I'm glad she's learning what justice looks like.

∞∽∞

I don't want to make it sound like we are out marching in the streets with the kids every weekend. We aren't. There are gymnastics classes and swim lessons and school projects and all the basic life stuff that has to be tended to.

But there are other ways to be an advocate.

Stay informed and engaged in the political process. Subscribe to your local paper and figure out whose district you live in. Pay attention. Show up.

Be aware of the global business practices of big corporations, and make informed choices about where you shop. American boycotts were what finally tipped the tide in the fight against apartheid in the 1980s. More recently, public pressure has led some stores to voluntarily offer employees more than the legal minimum wage. We don't have to be—and ought not to be—ignorant about how our choices matter.

Read up on an issue you care about, and let your elected officials know what you think. It's awfully overwhelming, I know, when you start thinking about all the issues out there, all the problems to be fixed, so maybe start small. Start with one thing that matters to you. Think of one person who matters to you—a neighbor, a family member, somebody at church—and figure out how they're affected by public policy. Learn somebody's story.

Listen to King Lemuel's mother: Look out for the vulnerable and give voice to the voiceless.

Sure, our democracy isn't perfect. But the thing about a democracy is that nothing changes until the people change—until we change. We, the people, is all we've got.

Well, that and hope.

Advocacy is hope in action. If we didn't think there was hope, we'd never do anything. If we didn't think anything would ever change, if we didn't think there could be a different way, then we'd all stay home in bed on Saturday mornings.

But we do. We hope. And so we take to the streets and lift up our voices and head to the voting booth, and we take part in the coming kingdom of God.

CHAPTER 12

DELIGHT

The power was out when we woke up this morning. I thought I'd heard the alarm but went back to sleep, and when I finally woke up, the clock was dark, and I had no idea what time it was. Panicked that Harper would miss the bus and we'd all be late, I kicked Rob and rushed into the kids' room to get them going.

The good news was that the power had apparently gone out just a few minutes earlier, because the coffeepot, which we'd set on the timer last night, was full and hot. A Wednesday morning miracle: hot coffee with no electricity.

But still, even with the caffeine, the lack of power made for a weird morning. It's still winter, and the sun wouldn't be up for another hour, so we dug through drawers in the dark, in search of matching socks. I skipped a shower and pulled my hair back into a ponytail. The kids were great, actually, jumping into the adventure and digging out their flashlights I made their lunches with a headlamp strapped to my forehead.

This was the second time in two weeks that we'd lost power, both times unrelated to a storm or high winds. "It's like we live in a third-world country," I almost said out loud before I caught myself, because it isn't at all like we live in a third-world country (and that's not even the right term anyway). We were certain the power would be back on in an hour or two, and we had plenty of batteries and candles. The outage had likely been caused by an accident or utility maintenance, not a war or a lack of infrastructure. And we had hot coffee!

The kids giggled through breakfast by flashlight, and we managed to all get ready in time. I was the first to leave, and the sun was coming up by then so the day felt more normal. I backed out of the driveway just as the school bus came up the street, so I sat for a minute and watched my family in the front yard. Harper running down the front walk to meet the bus, the backpack that looked so big on her a year ago now sitting securely on her shoulders. Rob on the front porch, holding Jonathan, who waved emphatically as the bus pulled away. Rob caught my eye and smiled, and then the two of them slipped back inside, on to the next task of the day.

Moments like that take my breath away sometimes: the sweet, easy goodness of this life.

How could I not delight in it?

⊙⌢⊙

There's a quote from author E. B. White that has been rattling around my head for some time now. In an interview later in his life, he was asked for some advice about living a good life, and he said: "If the world were merely seductive, that would be easy. If it were merely challenging, that would be no problem. But I arise in the morning torn between a desire to improve (or save) the world and a desire to enjoy (or savor) the world. This makes it hard to plan the day."[1]

"If the world were merely seductive, that would be easy": that is, if the world were simply full of good things, happy news, enjoyable ways to spend one's time—it wouldn't be hard to figure out how to live a well-lived life.

And if the world were "merely challenging," that would be easy, too (if not as much fun). We'd roll up our sleeves and get to work.

But the reality is that the world is both. It is immensely challenging; the needs of the world are great and overwhelming. And it is immensely enjoyable; the world is also full of beauty and wonder and incredible delight.

This does, in fact, make it hard to plan the day.

When I started this project, this was the dilemma at the heart of my question: how was I to enjoy and delight in the good things of my life when there is so much pain and heartache in the world? Can both pain and delight exist simultaneously? Can we both improve and enjoy the world that God has given us?

Finally, one friend, who has made it her life's work to improve the world, said to me, "I love life! Life is here to be enjoyed." She told me that though she respects those who have taken on a life of poverty in solidarity with the poor, that's never been her calling. "My role," she said, "is to enjoy life and all the gifts I've been given, and to work hard every day so that everybody else can do the same."

It's a delightful world out there, and I think we ought to notice. God noticed, at the end of each day of creation, what a lovely world it was: "And God saw that it was good." I think God intends us for just such delight.

It's easy—if not always easy to make time—to find awe and delight in nature: brilliant sunsets, vast oceans, magnificent mountain views. But I think we are called to also delight in the smaller, more mundane bits of our life as well.

A new pair of running shoes.

A load of fresh laundry.

A really good movie watched on a big screen.

The warmth of a sweater or a pair of jeans that fits just right.

Chicken on the grill on the first warm evening in spring.

FaceTime calls with my nieces and nephew.

Driving with the radio turned up.

Chocolate milkshakes.

A fresh pad of paper and a good pen.

Kettle corn. (Which I just recently discovered. Where has that sweet-salty amazingness been all my life?)

Sunflowers and snowflakes, Snickers bars and s'mores around a campfire. Orchids and Oreos. Baseball and rainbows and sweet potato pie. Playgrounds and Taylor Swift songs and good novels and vanilla lattes and movies with Robert Downey Jr. (Maybe that's just me.)

And the things we humans can do! Build a spaceship to take us to the moon. Talk by video to someone on the other side of the earth. Transplant a heart from one person to another. Learn languages. Make babies. Walk on tightropes. Write stories. Paint pictures. Discover electricity.

We are missing something if we don't pay attention to just how delightful this life is.

God didn't have to make the world such a delightful place. I think, God being God and all, that God could have created a world that was entirely utilitarian, that didn't contain an ounce of beauty, but God didn't. God created this entirely delightful, crazy, mixed-up world and invited us to live in it.

It's a broken world, too, of course. It is not all delight. Our joys exist alongside all the pain and heartache that life on earth entails, sometimes all in the very same moment. Just as the psalms call us to lament, so do they call us to delight: "This is the day that the LORD has made; let us rejoice and be glad in it," proclaims Psalm 118. Our lament at the brokenness of the world does not negate our delight at its beauty. Living well in this complicated world calls for working for justice and caring for neighbor, but it also calls for rejoicing with gladness at the day God has made.

Now, here's where things start to get tricky again. Because sometimes those things that bring us joy, those parts of the created world in which we find so much delight, are the very opposite for somebody else. We might delight in fresh produce in the middle of winter, but the farmworkers who weren't paid very much to pick it and ship it to us no doubt feel differently. We might delight in the fact that we can get in our cars and go anywhere we want, but our poor earth is groaning under the strain of too many resources used.

Sometimes there's a relatively easy answer to this: We can make an effort to buy fairly traded coffee so that when we delight in that first cup early in the morning, we can trust that the folks who worked hard to grow and harvest those coffee beans were paid a fair wage.

But there's not always a clear-cut answer.

Sometimes we just live with the tension.

Like our trip to Barcelona last summer. Every time I told someone we were going, I found myself justifying the trip, though no one asked me to defend it. "It's our tenth anniversary," I said, explaining. *A special occasion—it's not like we dash off to Europe all the time.* "We've been saving up for it for a while now." *We're responsible people, practicing good stewardship of our resources.* "I'm on sabbatical, so the timing works out." *I'm not even neglecting my work . . .* "My parents will stay with the kids." *. . . or my children.* And though no one ever challenged my decision making, I wanted to plead, *Please, tell me it's OK that we go.*

It wasn't a hugely extravagant trip—except for the fact that being able to travel overseas at all is a luxury—but it was a lot of money all the same. The reality is that a lot of hungry people could have been fed with the money we spent on plane fare alone. I don't know that I ever made peace with that reality, but I did, finally, decide that living life well sometimes means choosing delight.

I wonder if that woman who anointed Jesus with expensive perfume wrestled with that question (Matt. 26.6-13). The Gospel writers don't let us in on her inner thoughts, but surely she knew, too, that the oil could have been sold and the money given to the poor. Jesus lets her off the hook when the disciples complain, but who knows? Maybe she'd gone back and forth in the hallway before coming in with her alabaster jar, unsure even at the moment the oil poured out that this was the right thing to do. But then it was out, it was done, and the fragrance filled the room.

So we went to Barcelona. It was good to visit a part of the world where we'd never been, one that is rich in history and beauty and culture. It was good to be on vacation. It was good for the two of us to get away together, to share several meals in a row that didn't involve any spilled cups of milk. We toured old churches and climbed into the bell tower of the unfinished Sagrada Familia. We rode the funicular up to Montjuic and had almost as much fun saying the word "funicular" as we did taking in the views from the top. We bought cheese and bread at the market and made a picnic, and we had tapas almost every night. The bike ride we took along the beach on our last morning there will remain, I suspect, one of the favorite memories of my life.

The trip was a delight. We rejoiced and were glad.

CHAPTER 13

———————— ⟨♡⟩ ————————

A NEW SONG TO SING

Keepers of an Old, Old Story

Last spring, for maybe the first time in my life, I didn't go to church on Palm Sunday. I was away from home, visiting some friends who'd just had a new baby, and we went out for brunch instead. This was weird for me, but apparently, I'm told, people do this all the time on Sunday mornings. On the way to the restaurant, we passed a big church near the center of town. Worship was just ending, evidently, and families were streaming out of the church and heading to their cars. Most were holding palm leaves, which they had no doubt waved during the processional. I could almost hear the strains of the traditional Palm Sunday hymn, "All Glory, Laud, and Honor." I could imagine the shouts of "hosanna" as they told the story of Jesus entering Jerusalem.

I watched as a couple of kids swatted each other with their branches, laughing, and I felt a pang of longing; as much as I was enjoying the time with my friends, I realized I had missed the palm parade. Holy Week was starting and I hadn't been part of the story.

◌◌◌

Christianity has been around for a while now, and since about the fourth century, it's been the dominant religion in the West. For all the history of the United States, that's been true, despite the religious pluralism that has always been part of our country's story. So it's easy to forget that at the heart of it, the Christian story is a truly countercultural one. At the very beginning, in the first generations after Jesus, Christianity was originally a grassroots movement called "the Way," which mobilized marginalized people in the Roman Empire.

These days, sociologists of religion—and, well, just about everybody—talk about the decline of Christianity, especially in mainline Protestant traditions like mine. Church attendance is way down; most people consider themselves regular churchgoers if they show up at worship once a month or twice a year, and a lot of people don't go at all. The whole "spiritual but not religious" thing is real. We in the church spend a lot of time bemoaning this fact and a whole lot more time dreaming up what we think will get people to come back.

I'm pretty sure we're missing the point. The gift of this major shift in American religion—and it is a major shift—is that the church can be countercultural again. These days, you're probably in the minority among your friends if you are active in a church. That means that you've made an intentional choice to orient your life around this ancient tradition, and I think there's something to that.

The Christian movement was always supposed to be about pushing back against the empire, the systems that hold us hostage and keep us—all of us—from living the abundant lives God offers us. Now, when there's no expectation that you'll be part of a church at all, you can decide which story you'll live.

That's why it felt so odd for me to have missed the palm parade that day last spring.

Marcus Borg and Dominic Crossan offer a compelling account of the Palm Sunday parade in their book *The Last Week*. Perhaps, these two scholars suggest, there were two parades entering Jerusalem that day:

> One was a peasant procession, the other an imperial procession. From the east, Jesus rode a donkey down from the Mount of Olives, cheered by his followers. Jesus was from the peasant village of Nazareth, his message was about the kingdom of God, and his followers came from the peasant class. . . . On the opposite side of the city, from the west, Pontius Pilate, the Roman governor of Idumea, Judea, and Samaria, entered Jerusalem at the head of a column of imperial cavalry and soldiers. Jesus' procession proclaimed the kingdom of God; Pilate's proclaimed the power of empire.[1]

Today, we are living in an empire of our own making. It is an empire not unlike that of Pharaoh, in which we are all expected to produce faster, bigger, more. It is an empire not unlike that of the Romans, in which the poorest among us don't have a place at the table. The task before us, if we hope to live faithfully and well in this life, is to choose which parade we plan to join: the imperial procession that maintains the status quo as the gap between the haves and the have-nots widens? Or the one in which the crowd calls out to Jesus to come and save us—the one where we can imagine that something might change, where there might be hope?

And of course—as we've seen over and over again by now—it's never as simple as choosing one over the other.

We are, inevitably, part of both. Writer Marva Dawn says it like this:

> Christians understand themselves as citizens of two king-
> doms, for we can't escape our society, nor do we wish to
> withdraw from it since we want to minister to it. Instead,
> we live in our wealthy society and also in the kingdom of
> God, our parallel cultures. And in that parallel culture, we
> tell the stories of our meta-narrative, we sing our songs,
> we pray our prayers, we proclaim in worship the truth—
> until we know that truth so well that we can say to the sur-
> rounding culture, "We don't believe your lies anymore."[2]

Like it or not, we're participants in the imperial parade. The only way to counter it is to wave our palms and tell an old story and sing a new song.

∞∞

It is not inevitable that we continue living in a way that takes up too much space on our planet, that pits the interests of the wealthy few against the needs of the rest. There are other ways to live.

The new monastic movement—popularized by Jonathan Wilson-Hartgrove, Shane Claiborne, and others—is one way that people have made changes to the way they live together. In these community-living arrangements, people share resources, gather for meals and prayer time, and generally build their lives together.

There's something compelling to me about that way of life. I've often daydreamed about some kind of communal living that felt a little like a college campus, with shared meals and community connection. (Apparently this longing is hereditary: my dad told me recently that he'd been drawn to the idea of communal living when he was a young pastor serving a small urban church.) In the condominium where we lived before Harper was born, there were six condos on a shared stairwell. Everybody was single, except for Rob and me, which meant that there were seven people and six refrigerators. That always seemed a little nuts to me, but I never worked up the courage to ask our neighbors if they wanted to share.

While some aspects of that kind of communal living are awfully appealing, it's not the life everybody is called to. It's not for me and my family, at least not right now. And it's not fair to hold that up as the perfect standard or the only faithful way to live.

There are other ways of nurturing community so that we pay more attention to how our choices affect the rest of the world. One couple with young kids told me about how grateful they are for their neighbors, whose children play with theirs, who look out for each other. They talked about participating with their school's PTA and getting involved in local politics that affect the communities in which they live.

Another friend, as we were talking about how to make decisions about where to buy stuff, given the dizzying array of implications in each choice, said that she wished she had a group of people who would hold each other accountable. We imagined together what that would be like—maybe a group that met regularly to support one another and share ideas about how to best make a good, faithful decision.

It's clear that swimming upstream against the culture is easier to do when you have the support of a community.

For me, it's the community of the church that is finally the place where my life makes most sense. Ultimately, that's because the church is the keeper of the ancient stories that remind us of God's justice and call us to a new way of life.

That's why I go to church. It's not because the people are good to each other (though they are). It's not for the dessert table at potluck dinners (but you should seriously try these incredible blonde brownies called Carolina Chewies that a woman at my church makes). People are good to each other in other communities. Other groups have potlucks.

But where else do you hear Mary's Magnificat or Isaiah's cry? Where else do you get wisdom like Jeremiah's call to settle down and make a life wherever you find yourself? Where else do you hear about the manna in the wilderness or the loaves and fishes, or the rich young ruler or Zacchaeus and his sycamore tree?

Those are the stories the church holds dear, and the truth they contain is the hope that holds everything together: the truth that the empire will not win; that there is enough to go around; that we can, and should, change; that new life is possible; that a new world will come.

In those old, ancient stories we hear the strains of a new, new song—like the one Mary sings, or Hannah, or the author of Psalm 40, who writes:

> I put all my hope in the LORD.
>> He leaned down to me;
>> he listened to my cry for help.
> He lifted me out of the pit of death,
>> out of the mud and filth,
>> and set my feet on solid rock.
>> He steadied my legs.
> He put a new song in my mouth,
>> a song of praise for our God.
>> —Ps. 40:1–3 CEB

Somewhere, then, in all our discussion of simple living and buying responsibly and advocating for justice, we have to also be connected to the community of the church. It's not because a group of people gathering for worship once a week, telling stories and singing songs, is so life changing . . . except, well, it is.

Those ancient stories have everything to do with us, with our lives, with the lives of our neighbors. I have this quote from Eugene Peterson on a sticky note on my desk: "When we submit our lives to what we read in Scripture, we find that we are not being led to see God in our stories but our stories in God's. God is the larger context and plot in which our stories find themselves."³

Sometimes our stories are huge and too heavy to carry ourselves. Sometimes our stories seem so small, our problems so mundane. But the truth is that our stories — the tiny details of our lives and the vast realities of the world — are all contained in God's story, and we are invited to join in the song.

That's what I was longing for that day last spring when I missed the palm parade. I want to live a life that is oriented by this story: the story of the exodus and manna in the wilderness and the call of the prophets and a baby born in a stable and a table with a Passover feast and a palm parade and a cross and an empty tomb.

It's the story I want to live by.

It's the story that gives me hope.

It's an old story, but it's new all the time.

CᴆᴀᴆD

The week before Lent begins this year, I slip out of town for a couple of nights. It's been a busy season; I feel like I've been running on empty since Christmas, and as much as I love my family and my work, I need to be away from both for a bit.

This time last year, I was preparing for my trip to Nicaragua. I'm not going nearly as far this time, just north of town, where there's a Franciscan retreat center nestled in the woods. It's beautiful here, and quiet. I'm here midweek, so there are only a couple of other retreatants. I share meals with them, along with Father David and Father Louie, who run the place, but other than that, I'm on my own.

When I check in, I ask about Internet access. The woman who showed me my room gives me a look that is somewhere between apologetic and pitying, and she just barely refrains from rolling her eyes. "It's just for staff," she says, not unkindly, "just for administrative things." I take this in for a minute, and she goes on. "Sometimes, if you take your phone out to the side of the building, you get a signal. . . ." But her look conveys that she thinks I could probably survive for forty-eight hours without checking Facebook.

Later in the afternoon, I change into my running shoes and go exploring. On the hill behind the center, a stone path leads to a labyrinth and a chapel overlooking the woods, bright and new but containing the traditions of centuries of prayers. I walk the labyrinth for a few minutes, winding my way into the center and then back out. There's a rhythm to it, short paths leading to longer ones. In the middle, some other walker has spelled out the word *faith* with small stones.

I think of Walter Brueggemann's suggestion that keeping Sabbath is a way of resisting the call of the world to go faster and build bigger; on the surface, a labyrinth is an exercise in futility and inefficiency. You quite literally go around in circles, and it gets you nowhere. But of course, getting somewhere isn't the point.

I am grateful for the witness of this place, which reminds me that there is a different way to live. I leave the labyrinth behind and follow the trail into the woods. I've brought my headphones and intended to listen to a podcast while I hike, but instead I choose a different story. I walk in silence, the only sound the crunch of leaves and gravel under my feet.

CONCLUSION

My friend Becca, standing in my kitchen, helping get dinner ready: "Tell me more about your book."
Me: "Well, it's going to have a very unsatisfying ending."

I recently discovered that I'm a Type One in the Enneagram personality system, a typology of nine interconnected personality descriptions that seems to be all the rage right now. Rob and I had some friends over recently, and we all stayed up way too late sorting through our Enneagram types and laughing at how easily characterized we all were.

Being a One means I'm always looking for the right way to do something. I like to-do lists and rules and clear expectations. I have high standards for myself and other people, and sometimes (by which I mean almost always) I think I'm doing things right and everybody else is wrong. This probably makes me exceedingly fun to live with and work with. (Sorry, Rob and every colleague I've ever had.)

I like answers and finished projects.

When I described this book to people, when I said that I was exploring what it means to live faithfully with abundance in the face of inequality and injustice, I generally got the same response: "Great! Tell me when you've figured it out."

This will come as no surprise: I didn't figure it all out. As a One, this is particularly infuriating to me.

I wish I could tell you what the answers are to all these questions about living well. I especially wish I could tell you that I'd made all the "right" choices about living simply and money and owning stuff and advocacy and getting to know our neighbors. But I haven't. I've done a few things differently, and I've learned a lot since I started all this, but there's always more to do. And there's grade-school homework, and laundry, and Netflix, and I'm pretty much exhausted by the time the kids go to bed every night, so there's a lot that doesn't get done.

I don't say this to let myself off the hook. I don't think that "we do the best we can" is good enough. I mean, it is good enough. It has to be. But it also isn't. We have to do more.

So maybe there are no clear answers and no specific blueprint for living a faithful life. But there are some claims we can make, some truths we can name about how we live.

We can name that the world is good and that the world is broken.

We can trust that there is enough. We can pay attention to our how lives affect people and the planet and make responsible choices accordingly.

We can acknowledge the harm when our choices have negative impacts, even if there's no other good choice.

We can weep for the ways the world is broken.

We can delight and give thanks for what we have.

We can learn from our neighbors.

We can put our hope in God's promises.

We can participate in a tradition that tells us there's an alternative story to the one we are living.

We can live with the ambiguity of unclear answers.

We can love the world the best we can.

Last month, the front page of our local paper featured a story about hunger in our community, noting that the number of people who don't have access to healthy food was going up, while food-pantry shelves are regularly stripped bare.

A few weeks later, another article came out, celebrating the fact that the homeless population was going down.

Some things get better; some get worse.

Gay marriage is finally legal, which was almost impossible to imagine a couple of years ago.

Nine days before marriage equality became law, nine black people studying the Bible at church were massacred by a white man, the latest in a series of events that make it clear that the racial wounds in this country are deep and raw.

Some things get better; some get worse.

That night at the ice skating rink—when it looked like there weren't enough sleds but it turned out there were plenty if we just passed them up the line—I waited for Jonathan to go down the sledding hill for the umpteenth time and watched the other parents and kids interact.

One grown-up saw a child without a parent nearby, hesitating around the edges of the line, and encouraged her to start up the steps, assuring her that we'd pass a sled up soon. Another explained to an anxious parent that the sleds were coming and her kid would get a turn.

That's how it works, I thought. Somebody sees what's happening, notices the rising anxiety of the people around them, and then steps in to explain that there's enough. Or somebody notices an injustice—a kid won't relinquish his sled, so he ends up getting more turns than anybody else—and figures out how to make it right. If enough of us stop panicking and make sure everybody gets a turn, if we trust that there's enough to go around and act like it, if we listen to the wise, patient people who remind us that we need not be afraid . . .

We just might be OK.

I don't know if we've made it to the promised land or not. Some days, when the sun is shining and the kids are playing in the yard and their laughter floats in though the open window, it sure feels like it. Other days, or just about anytime I read the news, not so much.

So on those days when it feels like we're already there, when I can hardly believe the goodness of this life, I want to remember Deuteronomy 26. There, with the promised land in sight, the people of Israel are commanded to offer up their firstfruits, to remember the stories of their ancestors and how God brought them out of Egypt, to celebrate and give thanks for all they've been given.

And on the days when the news of the world breaks my heart, when it's clear that we've got so far to go, I want to remember the feast on the hillside, when there was more than enough fish and bread to go around. I want to remember the call of the prophet Isaiah to loose the bonds of injustice, and I want to be part of the work God is doing. I want to remember Mary's song, sung with perfect conviction and unfailing hope that the world will be made right.

That nothing is impossible with God.

May it be so.

NOTES

Chapter 2: Enough

1. Walter Brueggemann, "The Liturgy of Abundance, the Myth of Scarcity," *Christian Century*, March 24, 1999.

Chapter 3: The Complicated Life

1. Attribution for this quote is proving hard to track down; I've seen it credited to everyone from Mother Teresa to Elizabeth Ann Seton to Mahatma Gandhi.

2. Barbara Kingsolver, *Animal, Vegetable, Miracle: A Year of Food Life* (New York: HarperCollins, 2007), 342.

3. Valerie Weaver-Zercher, preface to *Living More with Less, 30th Anniversary Edition*, by Doris Janzen Longacre, ed. Valerie Weaver-Zercher (Scottdale, PA: Herald Press, 2010), 13.

4. Ibid., 35–90.

5. Tsh Oxenreider, "What Is 'Simple Living,' Anyway?," *The Art of Simple* (blog), February 25, 2013, http://theartofsimple.net/what-is-simple-living/.

Chapter 5: The View from the Sycamore Tree

1. Nathan Dungan was a keynote speaker at the "Holy Conversations: Money, Church, and Millennials" conference I attended at Brite Divinity School in Fort Worth, TX, May 21–23, 2014. I also spoke with him by phone on June 11, 2014.

2. Michael Lewis, "What Wealth Does to Your Soul," *The Week*, January 2, 2015, http://theweek.com/articles/441315/what-wealth-does -soul.

3. John R. Schneider also notices and reflects on this connection between the rich young ruler and Zacchaeus in his book *The Good of Affluence* (Grand Rapids: Wm. B. Eerdmans Publishing Co., 2002), 163–66.

4. Rebecca Todd Peters, *Solidarity Ethics: Transformation in a Globalized World* (Minneapolis: Fortress Press, 2014), 5.

5. Ibid., 6.

Chapter 6: Confession

1. Barbara Brown Taylor, *Speaking of Sin: The Lost Language of Salvation* (Lanham, MD: Cowley Publications, 2000).

2. James Baldwin, *The Price of the Ticket: Collected Nonfiction, 1948– 1985* (New York: St. Martin's Press, 1985), 400.

3. *The Book of Common Prayer* (New York: Seabury Press, 1979), 360.

4. Taylor, *Speaking of Sin*, 42.

Chapter 7: Blessing and Curse

1. Ellen Painter Dollar, "Original Sin and Throw Pillows: On the Ethics of Stuff," *Ellen Painter Dollar* (blog), June 30, 2014, http:// www.patheos.com/blogs/ellenpainterdollar/2014/06/original-sin-and -throw-pillows-on-the-ethics-of-stuff/.

2. Ibid.

3. Laura M. Hartman, *The Christian Consumer: Living Faithfully in a Fragile World* (Oxford: Oxford University Press, 2011), 22.

Chapter 8: Sabbath

1. Walter Brueggemann, *Sabbath as Resistance: Saying No to the Culture of Now* (Louisville, KY: Westminster John Knox Press, 2014), 10.

2. MaryAnn McKibben Dana's book *Sabbath in the Suburbs* (St. Louis: Chalice Press, 2012) addresses this very question quite well and in more depth than I can go into here.

Chapter 9: Stranger to Neighbor

1. The documentary movie *La Camioneta*, directed by Mark Kendall (Follow Your Nose Films, 2013), tells the story of one such decommissioned bus taken from the American Midwest to Guatemala and highlights some of the complications of these relationships.

2. A number of people have raised questions regarding the integrity of short-term mission trips. Here are some articles I found helpful: Brian M. Howell, David Livermore, and Robert J. Priest, "Should Churches Abandon Travel-Intensive Short-Term Missions in Favor of Local Projects?," *Christianity Today*, June 25, 2012, http:// www.christianitytoday.com/ct/2012/june/short-term-missions.html; Jamie Wright, "The Whole Can of Worms, at a Glance," *Jamie the Very Worst Missionary* (blog), December 16, 2011, http://www .theveryworstmissionary.com/2011/12/whole-can-of-worms-at-glance .html. Laurie Occhipinti also addresses these questions — and suggests a way forward — in her book *Making a Difference in a Globalized World: Short-Term Missions That Work* (Lanham, MD: Rowman & Littlefield, 2014).

3. Rebecca Todd Peters, *Solidarity Ethics: Transformation in a Globalized World* (Minneapolis: Fortress Press, 2014), 37.

4. Ibid., 40.

5. Ibid.

6. Samuel Wells, "Rethinking Service," *Cresset* 76, no. 4 (Easter 2013): 6–14.

7. Laura Jean Torgerson, "Do Something! But What?," *Century Blog*, March 15, 2012, http://www.christiancentury.org/blogs /archive/2012-03/do-something-what.

8. Wells, "Rethinking Service."

Chapter 10: Hope

1. Parts of this chapter were expanded from a blog post originally published on the *Christian Century* Web site, "Here Comes the Parade," December 10, 2014, http://www.christiancentury.org/blogs/archive/2014 -12/here-comes-parade.

Chapter 11: Taking It to the Streets

1. Except for my mother-in-law, of course, who is wonderful and gracious. Hi, Babs!

2. Doris Janzen Longacre, *Living More with Less, 30th Anniversary Edition*, ed. Valerie Weaver-Zercher (Scottdale, PA: Herald Press, 2010), 43.

3. *A Place at the Table*, directed by Kristi Jacobson and Lori Silverbush (Los Angeles: Magnolia Pictures, 2013).

4. This portion of the chapter was expanded from a blog post originally published on the *Christian Century* Web site, "My Daughter's Moral Monday Field Trip," June 5, 2014, http://www.christiancentury.org/blogs/archive/2014-06/my-daughters-moral-monday-field-trip.

5. William J. Barber II, *Forward Together: A Moral Message for the Nation* (St. Louis: Chalice Press, 2014), 159. Previously published in the May 2013 edition of *Sojourners* magazine.

Chapter 12: Delight

1. Israel Shenker, "E. B. White: Notes and Comment by Author," *New York Times*, July 11, 1969, http://www.nytimes.com/books/97/08/03/lifetimes/white-notes.html. MaryAnn McKibben Dana, whose writing has been influential in lots of ways, introduced me to this quote.

Chapter 13: A New Song to Sing

1. Marcus J. Borg and John Dominic Crossan, *The Last Week: What the Gospels Really Teach about Jesus's Final Days in Jerusalem* (San Francisco: HarperSanFrancisco, 2007), 2.

2. Marva J. Dawn, *Unfettered Hope: A Call to Faithful Living in an Affluent Society* (Louisville, KY: Westminster John Knox Press, 2003), 195–96.

3. Eugene H. Peterson, *Eat This Book: A Conversation in the Art of Spiritual Reading* (Grand Rapids: Wm. B. Eerdmans Publishing Co., 2009), 44.

CPSIA information can be obtained
at www.ICGtesting.com
Printed in the USA
FFHW021859171219
57042113-62637FF